Locked in – Locked out

The experience of young offenders out of society and in prison

Locked in – Locked out

The experience of young offenders out of society and in prison

Angela Neustatter

 CALOUSTE GULBENKIAN FOUNDATION, LONDON

Published by
Calouste Gulbenkian Foundation
United Kingdom Branch
98 Portland Place
London W1B 1ET
Tel: 020 7908 7604
E-mail: info@gulbenkian.org.uk
Website: www.gulbenkian.org.uk

ISBN 0 903319 88 8

British Library Cataloguing-in-Publication Data
A catalogue record for this book is available from the
British Library

Designed by Andrew Shoolbred
Printed by Expression Printers Ltd, IP23 8HH

Distributed by Turnaround Publisher Services Ltd,
Unit 3, Olympia Trading Estate, Coburg Road,
Wood Green, London N22 6TZ
Tel: 020 8829 3000, Fax: 020 8881 5088
E-mail: orders@turnaround-uk.com

Photographs by Olly Hoeben

Contents

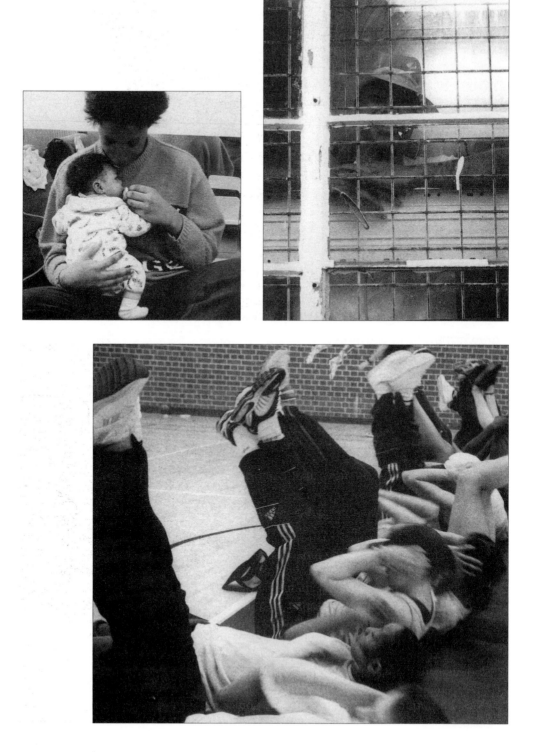

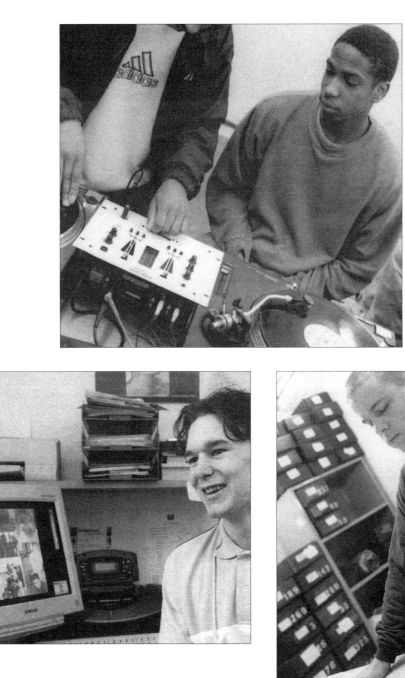

Author's acknowledgements

My thanks go first and foremost to the young prisoners whose voices and stories are at the heart of this book. I am grateful too to the prison officers and governors who gave me their time and assistance, and to all the other people working with young offenders whose words illuminated aspects of my research.

I owe particular thanks to Sir David Ramsbotham, who as HM Chief Inspector of Prisons was more than generous with his time.

Una Padel at the Centre for Crime and Justice Studies was exceptionally helpful, as were prison ethnographer Anita Wilson and lawyer Mark Ashford, who carved out time he could ill afford to discuss the youth justice system with me. Juliet Lyon, Finola Farrant and Joe Levenson at the Prison Reform Trust were ever-willing to find information and give guidance at short notice. Frances Crook, Fran Russell and Charlotte Day at the Howard League for Penal Reform have been generous and enlightening with information, thoughts and comments throughout the project. Richard Garside at Nacro provided valuable facts and insights. Marian Liebmann commented helpfully on the final text.

I am indebted to Michael Little of the Dartington Research Unit, Kevin Browne at the University of Birmingham, David Utting at the Rowntree Research Foundation, Chris Tchaikovsky, director of Women in Prison, Andrew Coyle, director of the international section of the Centre for Crime and Justice Studies, John Harding, former head of the Inner London Probation Service, who has also been kind enough to write a foreword, Dr Eileen Vizard at the Institute of Psychiatry, Adrienne Katz, director of Young Minds, Deb Coles at Inquest and Melody Wimhurst, who all gave me time and the benefit of their research. Many thanks also to Ruma Multani in the Prison Service press office for the great help she gave in setting up my initial prison visits and to Steive Butler, arts coordinator at Huntercombe, for her considerable assistance.

YOT managers Larry Wright and Brendan O'Keeffe made room in very busy schedules to discuss the recent youth justice reforms. Ian Ross, director of Outside Chance, spent time describing the difficulties facing young prisoners on release. Trevor Philpott, director of C-Far, a training programme for released young offenders, proved exceptionally helpful.

I am most grateful to Ruth Cadby and Kyran Joughin, who transcribed many of my interview tapes and, as they became familiar with my subject, gave interesting and often illuminating comments and insights. Sarah Wedderburn helped me with background research with her characteristic rigour, and has my heartfelt thanks.

Nor should I forget the many friends and members of my family who have listened to me patiently as I talked to them ad infinitum about this most engaging and politicising of subjects. Their interest and support has been truly invaluable.

I owe particular thanks to Felicity Luard, my editor at the Calouste Gulbenkian Foundation, for the enormous amount of time, trouble and care she has given to this book. Sarah Salmon, as our adviser on the text, not only contributed her knowledge of the law on children and young offenders in the criminal justice system, but was a delightful and valued colleague.

Foreword

Just occasionally, maybe once or twice in a decade, the general public is stirred to take some responsibility for what is happening in our prisons, through a film documentary like the BBC Strangeways prison series, directed by Rex Bloomstein, or a published inquiry, such as Lord Justice Woolf's following riots in the same prison in 1990. Other writers, too, like the late Tony Parker, have helped us listen to the voices of the most marginalised of prisoners, be they sex offenders, homeless vagrants or lifers, without passing judgement or providing superfluous commentary.

Now Angela Neustatter joins their ranks with front-line reports on the experience of young offenders under the age of 21 on remand and under sentence in young offender institutions in England and Wales. As an experienced journalist she knows her craft well; she listens acutely and conveys through a fluent, balanced and intelligent script that she under-stands young offenders, their often miserable backgrounds and their lack of self-worth. But the picture she portrays is not one-sided; she speaks equally clearly for those publicly paid staff who take responsibility on our behalf for the rising total of young offenders, nearly 11,000 in September 2000, in custodial institutions. She records their hopes and frustrations, often in beleaguered situations, as they attempt, in the late Baroness Wootton's crystalline words, to look after 'other people's children' not their own.

As an outsider to criminal justice circles, her critical starting point is a question for government and those who pass sentence. Why do we send so many young people to prison, especially since the majority, 80%, are con-victed for non-violent crimes? Why, too, she asks, do we dispatch the most vulnerable, ill-educated, poor and badly parented of our children to institutions, where despite the best efforts of staff they are likely to be bullied, racially abused, and, in the most desperate of cases, be prone to suicide, self-harm and further mental anguish? She discerns, rightly, a tension between the populist 'get tough' approach of tabloid editors acting in concert with some politicians, set against the government's espousal of Human Rights legislation and the United Nations Convention on the Rights of the Child, which states that imprisonment for a young person should be used as a measure of last resort and for the shortest appropriate time. Why, again, are we so out of step with our major European partners like France, which despite having a considerably larger population than England and Wales has half as many children in prison?

Ironically, we now have in place, through two major pieces of legislation, the Crime and Disorder Act 1998 and the Youth Justice and Criminal Evidence Act 1999, a range of community punishments for young offenders that vary in intensity according to the seriousness of the crime. Managed by Youth Offending Teams, these can match the educational opportunities and offending behaviour programmes in the best of our young offender institutions whilst keeping young offenders within normal developmental processes: the family, the school and the local community. The groundbreaking 1999 Act additionally introduces the Referral Order for first-time young offenders who plead guilty in court, giving discretion to a Youth Offending Panel of lay representatives to engage offenders in structured discussions with their parents and crime victims to find an appropriate way for them to make amends, through an apology or some form of community reparation.

In Neustatter's view, if community penalties were properly used by the courts young offender institutions could be reserved for the minority of violent young offenders who pose a risk of serious harm to others or whose sheer scale of offending demands sustained attention by properly trained staff in a contained situation. Given relief from overcrowding some poorly managed young offender regimes, of which there are still too many, could begin to emulate the vision and energy of Neustatter's best quoted examples like Huntercombe and Lancaster Farms. Much, of course, depends on the quality of leadership in such institutions and the Prison Service's ability to identify governors who are capable of creating and sustaining, over a period of years, a caring and supportive regime that respects young people and expects of them, in turn, that they take full responsibility for their lives and for their offending behaviour.

Neustatter also highlights the special problems faced by young offenders on release. Their reoffending rate within two years of release from custody is approximately 75%. Many of them are without the support of families, coming from collapsed backgrounds where they have been publicly parented in care. Those who are technically homeless on release, some

25%, are twice as likely to drift back into crime as those returning to more stable accommodation and family support.

Finally, what remains clear from Neustatter's penetrating analysis of these young people's needs is that the costs of resettlement – helping them find jobs and housing, and providing a continuous cycle of attention – have been underestimated in comparison with the exorbitant costs of custody. Surely a bigger investment at the sharp end of release might just serve to reduce offending and further victimisation amongst this highly troubled group of young people?

John Harding CBE

John Harding CBE is a visiting Professor in Criminal Justice at Hertfordshire University, a member of the Parole Board and a member of the Institute for Public Policy Research Criminal Justice Forum. He was formerly the Chief Probation Officer for the Inner London Probation Service. He has had a long-standing commitment to improving the quality of services for young offenders. He is a Trustee of the Young Builders Trust, a Director of Addaction and an Associate of RPS Rainer.

Introduction

My starting point for this book was learning that in England and Wales we imprison a greater number of children and young people under 21 than any other European country, and that we imprison children at a younger age than most other countries – 10 in England and Wales, eight in Scotland and Northern Ireland. It is a shocking record considering that the UK is a signatory to the UN Convention on the Rights of the Child, which requires that children should be kept out of prison as far as possible.

Having discovered these facts, I realised that I didn't know why we imprison so many of our young and had no clear idea of what happens to them once, with the state putting itself *in loco parentis*, they are locked into prison and out of society. Our information about young offenders (YOs) and young offender institutions (YOIs) is, inevitably, provided primarily by the media, which since the killing of James Bulger have tended to regard child and youth crime as titillating and newsworthy. Public antipathy is whipped up with talk of the growing threat that society faces from violent young criminals, which in turn strengthens public demand for tougher measures. On the other hand, the media also tend to focus on stories about grim conditions and untenable staff behaviour in YOIs, or on tragic cases of suicide or murder of young people in prison.

So, are custodial sentences used too frequently and sometimes inappropriately in dealing with convicted young offenders? What are or could be the alternatives? What are the best and the worst of the prison experience for young people? How can practice be improved to rehabilitate YOs more effectively and to reduce subsequent reoffending rates? I was fortunate in being given a grant by the Calouste Gulbenkian Foundation to write a book which considers these issues and will, I hope, help to improve the public understanding of what prison is like for young people. My aim was not to present a statistics-based study, but an experiential book, a view of YOIs by those inside. I particularly wanted to give a voice to young prisoners – so often written about but so rarely heard.

I visited Feltham, which has been criticised on a number of occasions by the former HM Chief Inspector of Prisons, Sir David Ramsbotham, most recently in his report for the Prison Service in July 2001. My visits took place in March 2000, and again in May 2001 at the invitation of deputy governor Paul McDowell after a new governor, Nick Pascoe, had just taken over. I also went to prisons which have received more favourable reports from the Prison Inspectorate. I visited six YOIs in all: Feltham in Middlesex, Huntercombe in Berkshire, Lancaster Farms in Lancaster and Moorland in Yorkshire for males, and Holloway in London and Styal in Cheshire for females. I interviewed an average of 10 young offenders in each institution and some others after they had left these and other YOIs (all names have been changed). I also interviewed and have quoted prison officers and governors; lawyers and others involved in different aspects of the youth justice system and with implementing the recent reforms; members of agencies that work with the Prison Service; members of organisations that campaign against prison for children, as well as those who believe it may, in some instances, be the only way of stopping a spiral of chaos and destructive behaviour. A number of the governors and other prison staff I spoke to have since moved on to different jobs or institutions; my observations and comments apply to the regimes and ideas I encountered at the time I visited.

The age range of young people locked up in YOIs, who form the focus of this book, is 15–20 years, whether as juveniles (15–17) or older young offenders (18–20). Younger children who receive custodial sentences are sent to secure units or secure training centres. Of the YOIs I visited, Feltham and Lancaster Farms both take juveniles and older young offenders, as did Holloway when I went to it – it still receives a small number of each although the young offender unit has been closed; Huntercombe now takes only juveniles and is phasing out the older age-group; Moorland and Styal now take only older young offenders.

Chapter 1 set outs how the youth justice system works and looks at recent youth justice reforms for under-18 year olds brought in by the Labour government following the Crime and Disorder Act 1998.

Chapter 2 examines who the young people are who end up in prison, what factors in their lives cause them to be 'at risk' of offending, and how the media encourage a particular view of young criminals.

Chapter 3 describes the beginning of the prison experience, what it is like to arrive at reception – delivered by van from the courtroom, the induction process, getting used to the regime and the prison environment, and relating to prison officers and peers.

Chapter 4 considers the situation of unconvicted young people remanded in custody, many of whom do not in the end receive a custodial sentence, and the possible alternatives to remand.

Chapter 5 looks at some 'wholly unacceptable' aspects of prison – racism, bullying, mental health problems, suicide and self-harm – and at the policies in place for dealing with these, and whether they work.

Chapter 6, by contrast, sets out to present a picture of best practice and of caring, constructive treatment of young inmates by governors and staff – a good ethos, a dynamic regime, effective education, living skills courses, drug treatment programmes – with a view to achieving something positive out of time inside.

Chapter 7 considers the issues that are particular to girls and young women in prison and whether there may be a case for a different penal approach to them.

Chapter 8 looks at the moment a young person is given his or her possessions in a bag and steps through the gates into the outside world; it assesses what preparation there is during the sentence for life outside and what support ex-YOs receive once they are back in society.

Angela Neustatter

'This is a turbulent and distressing period in the history of youth justice and the recent tidal wave of moral hysteria over youth crime is testimony to the power of media reporting in shaping official policy in highly sensitive areas.'

Dr Julia Fionda, School of Law, King's College, London

1   Tough on crime

Three weeks after his 15th birthday Liam, now 20, went to prison for the first time. He says: 'It was no surprise. I'd been in trouble since I was small … nicking … breaking into cars … I was known as a local menace.'

He has been back seven times since and his cool expression, the sneer as he responds ('do you want the violins version?') to a question about growing up with an alcoholic father and an emotionally battered mother who then divorced when he was eight, are part of what he has learnt inside. That, and not to trust anyone: 'I tried for a while. Now I have acquaintances, but I don't get close.' He stopped stealing in his mid-teens and began dealing in drugs although he is too fastidious to use them himself. This way he makes a good enough living to buy himself into the restaurants and bars where 'the people' go; he can afford good clothes, which he says is impossible on state benefit, and he hates looking down and out. He sits in a neon-lit room at Lancaster Farms prison where he is to serve out his latest two-year sentence.

Liam doesn't like the idea of spending his life in prison but nor does he see it stopping him committing crimes. He asks matter of factly: 'How else am I going to earn a decent living? Who'll give me a job with my record? I don't have a home, no address.'

He does, however, see a way he could get on to 'a straight road' and dreams of his plan a good deal as he lies in his cell. 'If I could make enough through crime to buy a house and rent most of it out so I had an income as well as a home then I could go straight. But first I have to get the money to buy the house…'

And it's not likely to happen, he says in the next breath. Meanwhile he has cost the taxpayer thousands of pounds for every year he has been inside. He is bright and quick-witted, and appreciates having learnt to read and write in prison education because it has enabled him to study psychology and become adept at 'mind games'. 'But what will I do with it? It's a shame someone didn't show me learning could be enjoyable a bit sooner, you never know I might have been in this place giving cognitive tests to the tossers I have to mix with now.'

If Liam's criminal trajectory as a juvenile had started after the April 2000 youth justice reforms it is possible that he might have been one of the young offenders the government has committed itself to dealing with in the community rather than in custody. Or he might have benefited from the large sums of money set aside for working with the youngest offenders in prison in the hope of altering their destiny. As it is, Liam is a repeat offender and with each prison sentence the likelihood of his being able to stop reoffending gets less.

Too many, too young

Locking up children and young people when they keep breaking the law may seem an effective way of showing them that they cannot get away with such behaviour, but the truth is that few of them bear that lesson in mind when they leave prison. Reoffending rates for children and young people under 21 who have served custodial sentences are consistently put at around 75%,[1] making custodial sentences for this group 'stunningly ineffective' in the words of the Children's Society. In fact, prison is slightly less effective in preventing youth crime than community punishments, for which the reoffending rate is 70%.[2] It is, however, vastly more expensive for the taxpayer, and at best is likely to be a negative experience and at worst a deeply damaging one. Despite this, in England and Wales we lock up more of our young in terms of numbers than any European country. (In September 2000 there were 10,713 under-21s in all penal establishments in England and Wales, including those on remand.)

A comparison with similar European countries to establish what proportion of the prison population are children also shows starkly how much more readily we imprison young people. In France in September 2000 there were 4,987 under-21 year olds in prison, equalling 10.2% of the prison population; in the Netherlands it was 941, equalling 6.8% of the prison population, while the figure for England and Wales, 10,713, was equal to 16.3% of the prison population.[3] And this is happening in a country that has ratified the UN Convention on the Rights of the Child, with its specific mandate to keep children out of prison because it is a wholly unsuitable environment for them.

In the UK we also criminalise our children younger than almost any other country, at an age when many of us see our own young as scarcely capable of deciding what they want for breakfast, let alone of understanding complex matters of morality. The age of criminal responsibility, meaning the age a child can be dealt with by the criminal justice system, is now 10 years in England and Wales, and eight years in Scotland and Northern Ireland. This means that children from the age of 10 (and eight) are now subject to the same laws as an adult.

Until 1998 the common law rule of *doli incapax* meant that a child aged 10–13 could be convicted of a crime only if it was possible to prove that they knew what they were doing was seriously wrong. Once convicted, they were subject to the punishments that were and are applicable to children of this age-group. But in 1998 it was decided that the principle of *doli incapax* was no longer appropriate because children of this age had become more sophisticated and worldly-wise. The abolition means that a child of 10 years and over can now be held to know that the act they have committed and are charged with was seriously wrong as distinct from merely naughty. But the onus remains, as ever, on the prosecution lawyer to show that the child defendant had the intention to commit the crime and to prove that he or she did indeed understand that what they did was seriously wrong.

The change in this ruling followed public outrage over the James Bulger case and a widely voiced belief that the two boys who killed the toddler fully understood the evil of what they were doing. So as the law now stands it is only up to the age of 10 (or eight in Scotland and Northern Ireland) that children are not held responsible for a crime, which means that they cannot be arrested or prosecuted when they commit one.

The crimes

In 1999, nearly half of all cautioned and convicted offenders in England and Wales were aged under 21 years.[4] A survey in 1998–9 showed that the average age when offending starts is 13 for boys and 14 for girls, while almost a fifth of 12–30 year olds admitted they had committed one or more offences in the previous 12 months (between October 1998 and October 1999).[5] The first part of this survey had been conducted in 1992–3, and in the intervening years there was a 14% increase in the percentage of 14–17 year old boys admitting to offences.

It is hardly surprising that such statistics may lead us to view young offending as a very real cause for anxiety. However, it is important to separate the just over 20% of convicted young offenders who are a real threat to society or each other because they commit violent crimes, including street fights and feuds, from the 80% who commit non-violent crimes, primarily property or car crimes, fraud or drug offences (see page 29). Of course these latter crimes can cause a great deal of suffering for the victims, but they are not the same as crimes of violence against the person and there are many reasons why prison may not be the most effective way of dealing with non-violent offenders.

There is also a difference in types of crimes committed depending on age. In the same 1998–9 survey, comparatively high rates of offending by 14–15 year old boys reflected their involvement in fights, buying stolen goods, theft and criminal damage. Boys aged 16–17 were a third less likely to cause criminal damage, and over a third of their offences involved fighting. Group fighting increased in the 18–21 age-group; shoplifting and criminal damage declined, but fraud and theft from the workplace began. The crimes of girls under 16 were, similarly, criminal damage, shoplifting, buying stolen goods and fighting. Over the age of 16 girls committed less criminal damage and shoplifting, although they were increasingly involved in fraud and buying stolen goods.[6]

After arrest

Once a young person is arrested, they are told their rights and taken to a police station, just as if they were an adult. Here the custody record will be opened, and if the young person is a juvenile (in this context under 17 years) an 'appropriate adult' – a person responsible for their welfare – should be informed of their arrest. The suspected offender will be interviewed. Following police investigation they will then be released or charged. If charged they appear in court where it will be decided if they are to be granted bail or to be remanded in custody, in which case they will be transferred to a secure unit or, if there are no places available, to a young offender institution (YOI).

Keeping them out of the criminal justice system

Keeping young offenders out of the criminal justice system is one of the central intentions of youth justice policy although, as critics are quick to point out, the number of juveniles placed in custody actually increased for a while after the introduction of youth justice reforms following the Crime and Disorder Act 1998. The reforms included a new sentence for under-18s, the Detention and Training Order (DTO), introduced in 2000 (see page 23). This sentence is spent half in prison and half in the community, and perhaps the courts saw it as a good way of showing the public that they were being tough on young criminals while at the same time giving them rehabilitation 'outside'.

Cautions have traditionally been the most widely used method of making a young person realise how serious their offence is and, hopefully, frightening them out of reoffending. It has proved more effective than perhaps most of us realise in preventing reoffending although that effectiveness diminishes each time it is used.

The condition of a caution used to be simply that the young person admitted guilt and agreed to being cautioned. The Crime and Disorder Act 1998 put the concept of cautioning, which had been non-statutory, onto a formal basis and introduced a hierarchy of penalties for under-18 year olds: for the first offence a young offender now receives a reprimand and for the second a final warning, which means what it says. The young offender must still admit guilt. If they do not they risk prosecution, and after a final warning any following offence should lead to prosecution although this decision is ultimately up to the police or, in some serious cases, is decided by the Crown Prosecution Service. A reprimand or final warning can also form part of a young person's criminal record.

The thinking here is that young offending needs nipping in the bud and a child or young person who receives repeated cautions may start thinking that they will always get off lightly, and have little incentive to change their behaviour. Barry Denton, while deputy governor at Moorland YOI, saw the problems this led to:

> 'I have kids inside who have committed 20–30 offences and only been cautioned, then one day the police say enough. The courts hear about the number of cautions given and the kid gets a fairly tough custodial sentence. A much earlier intervention with a community penalty would have been so much better.'

Youth offending teams and the youth justice board

When a young person aged 10–17 receives a final warning, they must be referred by the police to a Youth Offending Team (YOT). After conviction a YOT may be involved in either a community or a custodial sentence (see pages 21–3). The YOT is responsible for delivering a programme appropriate to each individual young offender. Programmes can include a variety of activities including reparation and improving school attendance as well as looking at offending behaviour. It may also involve the offender's family.

Local authorities with responsibility for education and social services are required to set up one or more YOTs in their area. YOTs are designed to be multi-disciplinary, bringing together a range of different skills and experiences relevant to young people's lives. So police, social workers, probation officers, someone nominated by a health authority and a person nominated by the chief education officer make up a team. The first YOTs were piloted in 1998 and Brendan O'Keeffe, a probation officer for more than 10 years, is manager of the Kensington and Chelsea YOT, one of the original pilots. He is optimistic that YOTs will in due course evolve a far more comprehensive way of understanding and dealing with youth crime than has been achieved in the past:

'Inclusion, seeing youngsters as part of their society, is what drives YOTs, whereas I would say the thinking before was that they are something "other". We started from the basis that views on offending varied between extremes. You had the "fallen angels who need tender loving care" thinking on one side and the "irredeemably bad so lock them up" thinking on the other. But by bringing a lot of different views and thinking together you move further on. The concept is based on the idea that agencies dealing with youngsters do so in disparate ways with different objectives and philosophies and they have beetled away without connecting – and bringing these together to create a coherent whole is the whole point of what we are doing.'

The national Youth Justice Board was established at the same time as YOTs and is a public body accountable to the Home Secretary. It consists of between 10 and 12 members with considerable recent experience of youth justice. The Board's role is to monitor how the youth justice system operates and to oversee the provision of youth justice services.

The youth court

Most under-18 year olds are tried and sentenced in the youth court where magistrates and district judges are trained to deal with this age-group. These courts have a wide range of sentencing options available to them ranging from community orders, reparation orders, action plan orders, curfew orders, probation orders, drug treatment and testing orders, through to detention. Youth courts try all but the most serious crimes but they have limited sentencing powers. In cases that are too serious for the youth court's powers an offender may be committed by the youth court to the crown court for trial or sentencing.

Reflecting the young age of defendants, proceedings in youth courts are different from those in adult courts. They are separate from adult courts; the public are not allowed in and a parent or guardian must attend for a child who is not yet 16. Reporting restrictions, which were extended by the Youth Justice and Criminal Evidence Act 1999, protect the young person's identity.

Sentences

The sentences that convicted young offenders receive can generally be divided into community and custodial penalties, although fines, discharges and reparation orders are in neither category.

Community penalties
These have been renamed under the Criminal Justice and Courts Services Act 2000.

Supervision orders are available for 10–17 year olds and place the child under the supervision of a local authority, a probation officer or a YOT. The order can be for up to three years and may have a condition of residence, or a night restriction requirement (curfew), or various other requirements.

Action plan orders were introduced by the Crime and Disorder Act 1998 with the aim of providing a programme for up to three months specifically designed for the individual young offender, aged 10–17 years, which will address his or her offending behaviour. Thus the plan will have a variety of components which may include reparation or education, and a report, generally supplied by the YOT and outlining the proposed programme, is required before sentence is passed.

Attendance centre orders apply to 10–20 year olds and require the young person to attend at a centre for a specified number of hours. The maximum number of hours is age-dependent but for the older age-group is a total of 36 hours with no more than three hours being served at any one session.

Curfew orders apply to those aged over 16 and are for up to six months. They restrict the young person's movements for between two and 12 hours a day.

Community rehabilitation orders (formerly probation orders) are for those aged over 16 and may run from six months to three years. Throughout this period the young person must maintain contact with their YOT supervisor or caseworker. This supervision is intended to encourage them to reform and refrain from reoffending. Specified activities or treatment – such as drug treatment programmes – may be attached to the order.

Community punishment orders (formerly community service) are also available for those aged 16 and over, and require the young person to undertake a specified number of hours of unpaid work (between 40 and 240 hours) which makes reparation to the community. For example this could be clearing river banks of rubbish or repairing park benches. A pre-sentence report is required and written by a member of the YOT and then a caseworker is allocated before the order can be made. This sentence can be combined with a community rehabilitation order.

Drug treatment and testing orders were introduced by the Crime and Disorder Act for those aged 16 and over and run for between six months and three years. These orders are considered suitable if the offender is a drug user who may respond to treatment, but can be given only if facilities are available locally. The court must review the order periodically after sentence.

An offender who breaches any of these orders may be recalled to court and can be re-sentenced.

Custodial sentences

There are three types of custodial sentence for under-18 year olds, two of which are for 'grave crimes'.

1. A new custodial sentence, the Detention and Training Order (DTO), was a key part of the youth justice reforms under the Crime and Disorder Act 1998 and replaced the pre-existing situation of detention in a YOI for 15–17 year olds and the Secure Training Order for 12–14 year olds. The DTO sentence is of a fixed length ranging from four to 24 months. Half is served in custody, the other half in the community. The custodial part can be served in a local authority secure unit, a secure training centre or that part of a YOI designated for juveniles. A YOT member appointed as supervising officer keeps contact with the young offender while they are in custody and then continues to work with them on release. A DTO can be given to 12–14 year olds if they are considered to be persistent offenders, although this term is not defined by the legislation. A DTO can be given to 12–17 year olds for any offence which could lead to an over-21 year old being imprisoned.

2. A Section 90, formerly known as a Section 53, is a fixed length of custody given, for example, for robbery, a sex crime or homicide.

3. Detention at Her Majesty's Pleasure is the equivalent of a life sentence given to an adult, e.g. for murder.

Custodial institutions

Once a custodial sentence has been passed the convicted children (10–17 years) and young offenders (18–21 years) are transferred to one of three types of institution.

Secure units

Local authority secure units (LASUs) take the youngest convicted offenders – children aged 10–17 years; there are currently 32 across England and Wales providing about 450 beds. These differ from youth prisons in being under the control of local authorities, although inspected by the Department of Health, and most importantly they are bound by the Children Act 1989 to put the welfare of their child inmates at the heart of their programmes.

Because of this, reformers believe that if juveniles are to be imprisoned they should only ever be sent to secure units. It is an ideal agreed by the government but the reality is that there are far too few places and so juveniles continue to be sent to YOIs.

Secure training centres

For children aged 12–14 there are secure training centres (STCs), which were set up to be punitive rather than therapeutic even though they are designed for small groups of children and the buildings are considerably less austere than most prisons. The first of these was opened in 1998 at Medway in Kent and there are now three, with plans for two more which will each accommodate 40 children. STCs are operated by the private sector, which caused considerable controversy at first. Medway was evaluated over a two-year period from April 1998 to March 2000 and was found to have had a difficult first year, with a high staff turnover, insufficient staff training, and poor offending behaviour programmes and inter-agency communication.[7] The report recommended that these new custodial institutions move toward a child-centred focus, and improve their liaison with community agencies. It found that significant improvements were made at Medway in the second year. Two social services inspections of Medway reported 'unacceptably high levels of restraint' in 1999, but an improvement in care and practice in 2001.[8]

Young offender institutions

In all there are 22 young offender institutions (YOIs) in England and Wales making up the prison estate for those aged under 21. Because boys and young men commit a far greater number of imprisonable offences than girls and young women, the majority of these institutions are for males which means that they are more likely than girls to be placed near to their homes.

Although all centres in the prison system housing 15–21 year olds are called young offender institutions, after the youth justice reforms of the Crime and Disorder Act 1998 the prison estate for under-21 year olds was divided into two parts, and 'juveniles' – the 15–17 year olds – must now be kept separate from the older 'young offenders' (YOs). Places for juveniles in YOIs are bought by the Youth Justice Board, which has been set up to manage 10–17 year olds going through the criminal justice system. Regimes for juveniles in YOIs should observe the conditions of the Children Act 1989, although they are not bound by them.

The division of the prison estate into younger and older groupings does reflect the belief that these two age-groups are at markedly different stages in their development and therefore have different needs which require appropriate regimes. Both parts of the estate are administered by the Prison Service and inspected by the Chief Inspector of Prisons. Nevertheless conditions are very variable, particularly in the young offender part of the estate. Reformers critical of the damage they say prison can do to often fragile and impressionable children and young people, argue that the rules governing the way prisons are designed and run make it extremely difficult for the standards of the Children Act to be maintained, even when governors and staff have the best of intentions.

Taking them out of society

Even among those most ardently opposed to custodial sentences it is agreed that some children and young people behave in a way that means they must be removed from society. Michael Little at the Dartington Research Unit voices this feeling: 'I think most people agree that some kids have to be locked up for their own safety and for the safety of others but nothing like the number we see put away at present.'

There may be a good deal of agreement on this, but there is certainly a conflict of opinion about where these juvenile offenders should be locked up. Successive governments have believed that prison was a suitable place. But organisations campaigning for children to be treated in a way that acknowledges the conditions laid down in the Children Act and in the UN Convention on the Rights of the Child argue that prison is absolutely unsuitable for vulnerable and impressionable adolescents. It is a view supported by Sir David Ramsbotham, former HM Chief Inspector of Prisons. He stated that he wished to see all children who are given custodial sentences removed from prison and put into secure units.

Not that secure units are necessarily an ideal environment for reforming young people who have gone as badly and sadly wrong as some of those appearing in this book. But as Michael Little, who with others has spent many years researching and writing reports on secure units,[9] as well as on child welfare, explains, secure units are almost always better than prison because they are smaller and have a higher staff-to-inmate ratio, psychological and child development theory are a component of treatment, and it is far harder for the damaging subcultures that so easily evolve in prisons to do so in these much smaller, more closely monitored groupings.

Concern with the kind of environment in which our young are locked away when they offend should not, however, detract from the importance of recognising the needs of the victims and potential victims of out-of-control youngsters whose behaviour may well be fuelled by drink and drugs. There is no reason why society should be expected to tolerate a real threat to its safety and well-being. So while it is clearly sensible as well as humane, given the lives many young offenders have lived, to look for the most constructive way of keeping them out of circulation until they can control themselves, protecting and supporting victims must also be part of the thinking. It is a view expressed often and emphatically by former prison governor David Waplington. He instituted a number of radical, inmate-centred reforms while running Moorland YOI, but he explained that this was not indulging the criminal at the expense of those against whom they had offended. Rather, he was convinced that by treating prisoners with humanity and respect he stood a better chance of protecting the next victim.

Reasons for and against imprisoning young people

Ideas on how we should deal with young offenders have swung over the past century between the punitive make-it-hurt school of thinking to that favouring a welfare-based approach. Deterrence has often been held up as a reason for imprisoning young people and the short-sharp-shock approach has at times been used as a way of trying to frighten young offenders out of repeat offending – for example, the so-named 'boot camps', introduced in the mid-1990s. The numbers imprisoned rose between 1994 and 1998, during the time Michael Howard was Home Secretary, in response to his belief that 'prison works' not because it rehabilitates but because it keeps young offenders off the streets.[10]

Those arguing against imprisoning children and young people point out that the majority of young offenders grow out of crime as they mature and start to have new goals such as work and creating a family. It is a theory supported by the fact that the peak age for male offending is 18 years and for girls 14 years.[11] Certainly offending declines after the age of 21, although the fall is sharper and occurs earlier in the case of crimes of criminal damage and violence.[12] The argument is that prison, with the damage it may do to a vulnerable and impressionable child or young person, is very possibly an excessive punishment, and the National Association for the Care and Resettlement of Offenders (Nacro), in a report in 2001, contends that prison may actually prevent young people growing out of crime by retarding the process of growing up. Certainly prison is known to institutionalise its young inmates so that they find it harder than they might otherwise have done to look after themselves, make decisions and take the initiative once outside; it may break bonds with family and community, and with employment if they had a job. Prison may also subject young offenders to brutalising treatment by staff or other inmates, offer them an education in crime and stigmatise them when they come out.

Nor, as we have seen, does locking up our young achieve the desired result. Reconviction rates among male young offenders reach 76% within two years and all too often they reoffend within weeks or even days of release.[13] Those working with young prisoners believe that the rate is actually considerably higher because many are not caught. Reoffending rates for such schemes as the Probation Service's Sherborne House, which young offenders must attend daily for a full day's activities and education, claim a slightly higher rate of success than YOIs have so far achieved in reducing reoffending.

On top of this prison is expensive, with each young inmate costing some £27,000 a year in prison for a young offender and £46,000 for a juvenile, while the cost is around £156,000 a year per child in a local authority secure unit. Campaigning organisations argue passionately that if such sums were put into working with families to support them much earlier on when children start to get into difficulties, and in supporting children at school when they need it, we would see far better results.

It is to be hoped then that the government's commitment to keeping children out of prison will mean more community interventions and less of what was seen in the first months after the DTO was introduced. The gloomy prophecy of John Harding, then director of the Inner London Probation Service, that the DTO would be 'a trapdoor to prison' initially came true with more children being imprisoned by magistrates and judges. So much so that in August 2001 Sir Norman Warner, Chairman of the Youth Justice Board, warned that juvenile prisons were becoming over-full. There were 3,395 children in custody compared with 3,206 a year previously, despite the fact that the number of serious offences committed by this age-group had fallen over the year. Lord Warner told magistrates, who were seen as having used the DTO too zealously for minor offences, to cut the number of short sentences given to 15 to 17 year old criminals.[14] He advised that more community penalties should be used – a reminder of the Youth Justice Board's goal of keeping children out of prison whenever possible.

The UN Convention and human rights

The UN Convention on the Rights of the Child, which has the best interests of the child as its primary consideration, is cited by many reformers as the yardstick by which we should decide how under-18 year olds are treated. In 1991 the United Kingdom became a signatory to the Convention, which contains a clear commitment to keeping children out of prison. As with other human rights legislation it is intended to protect children from inhumane and degrading treatment and punishment. Article 37 states that 'the arrest, detention or imprisonment of a child shall be in conformity with the law and shall be used as a measure of last resort and for the shortest appropriate time'. However, UN conventions are soft law and not binding so they are notoriously difficult to enforce. The Human Rights Act 1998, which incorporated into UK domestic law the European Convention on Human Rights of 1950, offers more hope of genuinely challenging malpractice.

There is conviction among reformers working for young offenders that prison is not the place to rehabilitate the vast majority. This view has been expressed to me time and again during the course of my research, by governors and prison officers. Indeed Paul Mainwaring, while governor at Huntercombe, one of the most progressive and impressive YOIs, put it this way:

'I do the best I can to offer young inmates something constructive out of the time they spend here and I hope this approach will prove to have better outcomes than the brutalising punitive regimes. But I am a realist and I know the majority of these kids will go out and reoffend for all sorts of reasons that we simply cannot address. So how can I argue that prison is right for them? If I were running a business that had the success rate I and other youth prisons have, then I'd be forced to resign.'

Which brings us back to Liam; in and out of prison in the five years since he was 15, he has cost the community some £100,000 and has not been reformed or rehabilitated. Given that his crimes are not dangerous, might not a constructive programme in the community, giving him the education he clearly values in prison without the institutionalisation and stigmatisation he believes has taken place, have been a better use of tax-payer's money?

NOTES

1. *Prison Statistics, England and Wales*. London, Home Office, 1999.
2. *Ibid.*
3. Council of Europe Annual Penal Statistics Survey. Strasbourg, 2000.
4. *Digest 4 Information on the Criminal Justice System, England and Wales*. London, Home Office, 1999.
5. C. Flood-Page *et al.*, *Findings from the 1998/99 Youth Lifestyles Survey*. London, Home Office Research, Development and Statistics Directorate, 2000.
6. *Ibid.*
7. Ann Hagel, Neal Hazel and Catherine Shaw, *Evaluation of Medway Secure Training Centre*. London, Home Office, 2000.
8. *Social Services Inspectorate Report of an Inspection of Medway Secure Training Centre*. London, Department of Health, 1999; *ibid.*, 2001.
9. Roger Bullock, Michael Little and Spencer Millham, *Secure Treatment Outcomes*, Dartington Social Research Series. Aldershot, Hants, Ashgate, 2001.
10. Speech made by Michael Howard at the Conservative Party Conference, 1993.
11. See note 1.
12. London, Home Office Research, Development and Statistics Directorate, 2000.
13. See note 1.
14. Youth Justice Board, Press Release, 22 August 2001; *The Times*, 23 August 2001.

'As soon as faces and histories are given to the young people who are steadily filling our youth prisons, one is left with an overwhelming sense of the hopelessness and wretchedness of their prospects.'

Helena Kennedy QC

2 Demons or victims?

Who are the young offenders we lock up in such large numbers? Sir David Ramsbotham, former HM Chief Inspector of Prisons, observed that 'few subjects engage public attention and anger more than the criminal behaviour of young people'. Yet this 'engagement' is often the end of it. We are shocked by the statistics and stories in the media, but are not eager to know more about the individuals even though each child and young person locked up and locked out of society has a story and a history. If society is to play a part in preventing youth crime it would helpful to understand the circumstances linked to young offending. Young people who are troublesome are also very often troubled.

A perception of violence: the politicians' response

Violence by the young is very frightening and David Blunkett, when he was made Home Secretary in 2001, spoke out in the same emphatic way as his predecessor Jack Straw on his intention to crack down on violent crime. But while crime figures show a rise in violence and much is made of the increasing threat posed by the young, the proportion of convicted young people committing violent crimes remains around 20%. In June 1999, out of a sentenced prison population of 8,343 male and female 15–21 year olds in England and Wales, 1,833 had committed a crime defined as violence against the person (22%).[1] This could indeed be murder or manslaughter, for example a frenzied knife attack in which the victim dies, but it may also be a punch-up outside a pub after an argument which results in injury.

It is paradoxical that while politicians believe they can win votes by demonstrating that they will be, in Tony Blair's memorable phrase, 'tough on crime and tough on the causes of crime', society does nothing to reduce the graphic violence, frequently aggrandised and fed to our young as a regular diet by the entertainment industry. Cinema and TV know that box office success equates with ever more vivid and detailed depictions of violent acts and of course these are increasingly easily accessible to children of all ages, regardless of their psychological state. There is no absolute agreement on the impact of this but several studies have concluded that a continuous diet of violent images may contribute to a potentially serious desensitisation of children.[2] It may also lead to children behaving violently themselves, particularly when they have no other more constructive and rewarding stimuli to balance the violence they see as entertainment.

A view from the media

The media are the filter through which we learn much of what we know about young criminals, media that have become increasingly sensational-ist and interested in stories that have shock appeal, as youth crime – particularly when it is violent or depraved – certainly does. On the other hand these same media reflect and in some cases support or urge on, politi-cians who believe they must be seen to take a tough and punitive line on young offenders. To a large extent, the media mould and influence the way we see these transgressors and encourage a view of them as menacing alien others without individual character or values. This view is reflected by even such a thoughtful and compassionate journalist as Anne McElvoy. Writing as a columnist for *The Independent*, she described her reaction to a '... young peaky-faced male, his face half obscured by the hood of his T-shirt' lurching in the direction of her childminder on the pavement, 'his face expressionless, his eyes glazed'. She admitted to feeling guilty at assuming he was not to be trusted but went on: 'We know the faces of Britain's lost boys – the pinched, underfed visages whose numbers disap-pear from the system after school or even earlier, who are jobless ... They are sustained by crime or its proceeds, often drug-dependent and often drug-dealers. They father children they will never know, let alone care for. The only contact they have with social institutions is likely to be with courts or prison.'

However true this may be of some young men with peaky faces and glazed eyes sporting fashionably hooded tops, it is not true of all. And, importantly, a range of studies has shown how crime reporting in the media, with the degree and quantity of violence it suggests, is at odds with reality.[3] Yet the stereotyping of young men, and increasingly young women, as threatening, is widespread and pervasive. They have come to be labelled as louts, yobs and hooligans pretty well regardless of whether they have slipped a pack of beer under their jackets in a supermarket or battered someone to death. Jack Straw as Home Secretary articulated the notion that one young offender is indistinguishable from another when he declared that young criminals are 'ruining the lives of communities', thus packaging them all as a homogeneous group. The irony is that such stereotyping may actually play a part in leading to offending. Jock, 17, is serving a sentence at Moorland Young Offender Institution for shoplifting:

> 'I grew up in a rough part of Birmingham. I had my hair shaved and a group of us we went around being loud and talking tough. It felt good but we didn't do anything wrong, only people acted like we did all the time. We were always being told to get off the streets by cops and when we went into the shops in the nice bit of town you just knew there was a security guard following. That made me angry. I felt judged as a bad lot and it didn't matter that I'd been brought up well. My Mam was dead strict with us. One day after this security bloke had been like my shadow I thought, "Well I'll show him then. I'll see if I can get away with it under his nose." When his back was turned for a minute I nicked something. It gave me a buzz and I thought, like, so now I'm as bad as they think and I don't care. I went on doing it and as you see I got caught in the end.'

Class bias
Media reporting of crime also comes with a class bias. It is quite usual for a middle-class child or young person who enters the criminal justice system to be referred to as 'from a good home' and to have their school mentioned if it is a prestigious one, as happened with a young man sent to prison for his part in city riots. The press emphasised that he went to a public school rather than describing him as a lout or hooligan. A handsome middle-class young man accused of rape and later acquitted was portrayed as the good-looking victim of circumstance, whereas when the media deal with young people from underprivileged backgrounds the material is usually presented in a way that suggests guilt rather than making it clear that they could similarly be victims of injustice. The case of a teenage boy in a high-profile case where he murdered his mother was written about with a mass of quotations from friends and relatives saying what a shock this was in such a quiet, well-mannered and respectable boy from a strict middle-class home.

The class bias in the media reflects the reality of what may happen when a child or young person from a 'good' home gets into trouble. They are less likely to enter the criminal justice system in the first place by being arrested and charged when caught by the police than those – the vast majority of young people in prison – who come from the working classes or so-called 'underclass'.[4] Self-report studies in which young people who are not necessarily in trouble are asked about crime show that middle-class children are as likely as their disadvantaged peers to have been involved in some kind of illegal activity.[5] Mark Ashford, who specialises in legal aid work with young offenders,[6] knows well that middle-class children are less likely to be charged, remanded in custody or sent to prison than their less privileged counterparts:

> 'You get magistrates who spot within minutes that they have a middle-class defendant and their attitude changes straight away. They apologise to the defendant and family for having had to wait, that sort of thing. And if you are defending you play on that saying "Oh, your worship, he's devastated by what he's done." And it goes right the way through.'

Added to which, Ashford says, young people who cannot afford to choose their lawyers but are allotted one on legal aid, may well get someone who has little enthusiasm: 'Working with children is low-status work and it's seen by many as a way of getting experience needed to move on. So in a way these young defendants are treated as disposable.'

I need wicked trainers too

Millions of pounds are spent annually on marketing to young people such commodities as mobile phones – and teenagers are now mugging each other as well as adults for these – fashionable clothes, shoes and gear at prices that many know they are unlikely to be able to afford. But the fact that a sizeable section of the population cannot hope to earn the sums required for the latest phone, designer clothes, trainers with the right logo, musical equipment, CDs or tapes does not mean they feel the desire for these things less keenly.

Mikie, 17, at Moorland, one of five children whose father died when he was 11, talks of living in poverty as meaning they had little to eat, a bath once a week and a mother who was constantly stressed and talking of them 'going under'. For him trainers became a symbol of how different he was from other children he met at school:

> 'Always having second-hand clothes, never being able to be cool with other kids, that really affects you. And trainers, man, they really mattered at school. You were a loser if you didn't have wicked trainers. My Mum she tried her best for us but she couldn't do £50 trainers – no way. And I used to see all the older guys driving around in BMWs wearing gold chains, leather jackets and designer gear and it made me feel I had no hope of ever belonging. Robbing was the only way so me and others like us used to go down the arcades, to the gambling

machines and we won a bit there but then we wanted more so we started taking from shops and it went on from there. At sixth form there was a gang of us and we started getting people down an alleyway and robbing them.'

Young men, who account for the bulk of youth crime, may also be demonstrating how little room they see for themselves in today's society where traditional male roles are so altered. Angela Phillips, who has written extensively about boys, makes the point that:

'Our politicians like to look at lawlessness, rioting, the destruction of communities, as a simple matter of bad behaviour and moral fibre. But … the reality seems to be that an increasing number of young men no longer believe they have a stake in society, and if they don't belong inside the society that created them, why should they respect its rules?'[7]

Those at risk

When we look into the environments and lifestyles of the young who end up inside there are certain common circumstances and events that appear to influence young people and predispose them to antisocial and criminal behaviour. Those who have identified these factors do not see them as a direct cause but stress that it is important that we see how influential they may be in tipping behaviour towards delinquency.

These factors include poverty, bad and unsafe housing, sexual and emotional abuse and physical violence. Neglect, ineffectual and inconsistent parenting, teenage and single-parent families, broken homes, family discord, large family size and family criminality are also known to add to the risk of antisocial behaviour. Spending time in care, exclusion from school, low educational attainment and particularly illiteracy as well as negative peer pressure also appear to have a significant impact on offending. Children may be able to withstand one or two of these negative circumstances but when their lives are shaped by a cluster of them it appears that conscience, empathy with others and the will to be social-minded frequently break down.

That said, not every child exposed to even a cluster of bad circumstances and life events goes wrong. Children of a particular temperament or psychosocial make-up will be more predisposed than others to behaviour that leads them into trouble. Impulsivity, lack of restraint, paranoid reactions and aggressive responses are correlated with delinquency, as are learning difficulties, hyperactivity and cognitive impairment, especially of verbal and planning skills. These clearly add to the difficulties of children growing up in adverse environments.[8]

Poverty

Poverty is defined as living on an income of less than 60% of the median and represents the overarching adverse circumstance. For poverty is not just a shortage of money but a condition that colours and corrodes, shaping life with anxieties and stresses, denying pleasure. It is the unchanging, seemingly unalterable state of living at the lowest level of survival.

During Mrs Thatcher's time as prime minister the number of children growing up in poverty rose from one in four to one in three. A report by UNICEF in 2000 showed that Britain has one of the highest rates of child poverty in Europe, a shocking fact that Prime Minister Tony Blair has promised to address.

Janine Morris, while deputy governor at Feltham, saw it simply: 'Most of the young coming here have the worst economic conditions, the worst housing, worst schooling and all too often ghastly home situations. And when the courts send them they blame us if we don't sort them out.' David Thomas, governor at Lancaster Farms, makes the point: 'It isn't everyone who comes from an inadequate social background who ends up in prison. But turn that the other way around and it is almost always the case that children who come here are from inadequate social backgrounds.'

This was what I heard, over and over again as I listened to children and young people inside telling their tales of lives spent in deprivation and chaos with parents who either could not or would not take care of them. Those who told a different story were the exceptions. And whereas most of us have goals, aspirations and possibilities offered to us when young, these inmates had no sense that they could achieve anything likely to win them approval or respect, let alone a decent living or a chance to change their circumstances for the better.

Children, when asked, say that growing up in such conditions has influenced their route to crime. Seeing their families struggling to manage was hard for them and many felt a kind of impotent shame at being unable to help.[9] Indeed shame is a word that prison governors use often when describing the way their young inmates talk about how they view themselves. Not shame for their crimes necessarily, but at who and what they are. As one governor says: 'They know they are regarded by the world around them as bottom of the pile. It may not be their fault but they feel it is.'

Tracy, 17, in Holloway for assault, puts it this way:

'Nobody comes to our estate who doesn't have to. And who's gonna send their kids to the stinking schools we go to? We don't see no toffs unless we go into their streets. You don't exactly get them popping in to have a cup of tea with me Mum.'

Ben, 18, in Lancaster Farms for aggravated burglary, takes satisfaction in forcing people who usually 'blank' him to take notice of him by stealing from their homes:

> 'If I went to the kind of houses I nick from and tried to speak to the people living there you know what they'd do? They'd tell me to f*** off, but when I've got their gear they have to take notice of me. I know they'll be stamping around the police station wanting to know what little bugger got into their home. That gives me a buzz.'

Mark, 18, in Moorland for aggravated burglary, illustrates how too many 'bad' things happening in life leave a child feeling stripped of the normal restraints and how the desire to be law-abiding becomes distorted.

> 'We lived in a very rough area of Manchester and my Mum well she didn't seem to give a f*** about me – once she moved this geezer in when I was eight. She'd been good to me up until then. My Dad died when I was 18 months. I started staying out all night, mixing with a bad crowd and by the time I got to 12 I was well off the rails. Nobody could control me. I did a lot of crime.'

Cared-for children

A very high proportion of children who end up in the criminal justice system have spent time being cared for by the local authority, sometimes because their parents cannot or do not care for them, sometimes because they get into such trouble that they have to be taken into public care. Feelings of abandonment and rejection, and also of being so bad they had to be sent away, are common.

Maggie, 17, is in Styal for a drugs offence. She was 'about nine' when her parents put her into care: 'My Dad and Granddad used to come into my bed at night and do things I didn't like so one day, when I was eight, I told my Mum. She called me a dirty slag and told me to get out. I was put into care.'

Local authorities attempt to find foster homes for such children. It is not surprising, however, given the number of serious personal problems many bring with them and the fact that they may well feel hostile and have difficulty in trusting adults, that foster home placements often do not work out. Living in local authority homes these children all too easily form allegiances and begin their criminal careers.

Doug, 20, was 12 when his mother died. His father quickly remarried and Doug disliked his stepmother intensely. He put himself into care but repeated foster home placements broke down. He had been doing well at school but with more than seven moves he lost interest. He got engaged at 18 but his fiancée died. It was then that he experimented with drugs and quickly became addicted to heroin. He has just left prison after a two-year sentence.

> 'I had a job for a while and earned the money for my drugs, but then I lost that and, it's the usual story, I was desperate. One night I broke into a chemist but I got caught. Looking back perhaps I should have gone to my social worker and asked for help to detox because I knew I should kick the drugs, but I didn't like her and she was angry with me because my placements kept breaking down.'

Out of school

If a child is out of school their chance of entering the criminal justice system rises considerably. Many young offenders told me that it was when they truanted or were excluded from school that they began getting seriously into crime.

Benny, 16, describes how within days of 'bunking off' from school he had begun shoplifting:

> 'I wanted some fags and to go to the gaming hall, but I hadn't any cash. My mate suggested we go to one of the big stores in the West End and help ourselves. I'd never done it before and I was nervous but my mate showed me how you keep a good eye out and just pause and look at something like a leather wallet, or if you can a watch or summat, and just slip it up your sleeve. No, it's not difficult to flog the gear if it looks class.'

Suliman, now 20, who completed two and a half years at Lancaster Farms for robbery and has 'kept straight' since he left 18 months ago remembers:

> 'I began taking rubbers from kids' desks at school and graduated to chocolate bars in newsagents. Once I knew I could do it I moved on to something more dangerous, more challenging and where I'd make more money. I was getting radios and the like from big shops before I got caught. I was out of school and the first thing I'd think about when I woke up in the morning was how I'd get my money.'

On the streets for long hours of the day these children and young people meet up with others in the same situation and often this is how their criminal activities begin. Boys in high delinquency areas reported being introduced to crime by the gangs they mixed with. In many cases crime begins as a response to boredom because the young people want money to pay for entertainment. Once excluded from school they get little education so prison juvenile units and YOIs are top-heavy with children who have scant education and often cannot read or write.

Parents

Many young offenders have grown up in single-parent families; a good number are illegitimate, and the proportion of such births is rising. A number of studies have shown that a one-parent family, with the greater likelihood of poverty and the additional strain of a parent trying to cope alone, correlates with delinquency, although it is also important to say that plenty of single mothers on very low incomes do a good job of parenting children who do not turn to crime. Among the young offenders inter-viewed here were a number whose lives in impoverished single-parent families, where the fathers had never been part of the picture, had shown no interest in their children or had walked out, had clearly been stressful and chaotic. For all that, many spoke with determined loyalty of the parents who had been there.

Peter, 20, in Lancaster Farms for the third time, says:

'I was your average little sod. I'm the big I am and nobody matters and I can't blame my Mum. She was a bit down after my Dad went, drank a bit too, but she tried disciplining me and getting me to go to school. I didn't want to know so that was my doing and the result is I've ended up here and it's certainly not my Mum's fault.'

Growing up without a father, or with a father who was alcoholic, violent, and emotionally absent, as so many of the young people I talked with had, meant there had been no constructive male role model for them. The con-versations I had with them echoed the words of Jim, 19, who had served time in a variety of YOIs:

'Dad lived at home but he never wanted to spend time with me. Mostly told me not to bother him. No, he didn't play football or tell me about the world and the only time he seemed to come alive was when he'd been drinking but that was singing and shouting not playing with us. Sometimes I'd look at the Dads in the soaps on TV or in the movies all into their kids and laughing and having fun with them and wonder what that was like. It made me dead sad when I was little but now I don't care.'

There are few things worse for a child than experiencing violence at the hands of the people they might expect to love and care for them. Yet parental violence is consistently reported by young offenders in prison. Listening to them it is clear how easily treatment that may possibly be undertood as normal discipline – angry words and smacking – can lead to more serious brutality and abuse: 'Sexual abuse and physical abuse are usually preceded and accompanied by psychological and emotional abuse

… verbal assault, including threats of sexual or physical abuse, close confinement, such as locking a child in a room, and … withholding food.'[10]

A number of studies have shown a link between harsh and aggressive parental discipline and children themselves becoming violent. In a sample of Section 53 (now Section 90) young offenders – those convicted of very grave offences – it was found that 40% had experienced beatings, kickings and a variety of other forms of physical harm or torture repeated in daily life.[11] Campaigners against the smacking of children see it as an intolerable excuse to use violence on children and the way children themselves are taught to become violent. Young offenders with low self-esteem have often been victims of different forms of violence at home or at school by peers.[12] The result is that, on the one hand, they feel ashamed of having allowed it to happen and, on the other, they are determined to prove they are not victims and so go on to bully when they get the opportunity, and to equate violence with power.

NOTES

1. *Prison Statistics, England and Wales*. London, Home Office, 1999.
2. *Children and Violence: Report of the Commission on Children and Violence convened by the Gulbenkian Foundation*. London, Calouste Gulbenkian Foundation, 1995.
3. Robert Reiner, 'The Rise of Virtual Vigilantism: Crime reporting since World War II', *Criminal Justice Matters*, No. 43, spring 2001.
4. John Muncie, *Youth and Crime*. London, Sage, 1999.
5. J. Graham and B. Bowling, *Young People and Crime*, Home Office Research Study 145. London, Home Office, 1995.
6. Mark Ashford and Alex Chard, *Defending Young People*. London, Legal Action Group, 2000.
7. Angela Phillips, *The Trouble with Boys*. London, Pandora, 1993.
8. Michael Rutter, Henri Giller and Ann Hagell, *Antisocial Behaviour by Young People: The main messages from a major new review of research*. London, Policy Research Bureau, 1998.
9. Juliet Lyon, Catherine Dennison and Anita Wilson, *Tell Them So They Listen: Messages from young people in custody*. London, Home Office, 2000.
10. K.D Browne and I. Fereti, 'Growing up in a Violent Family', in *The Child in the World of Tomorrow: The next generation*, ed. S. Nakou and S. Pantelakis. Oxford, Pergamon Press, 1997.
11. See note 2.
12. Adrienne Katz and Ann Buchanan, *Leading Lads*. East Molesey, Surrey, Young Voice in association with the University of Oxford, 1999.

'More damage is done to immature adolescents than to any other type of prisoner by current conditions. The vast majority of young people in custody need individual attention given to the problems which produced their criminal behaviour.'

Sir David Ramsbotham, HM Chief Inspector of Prisons

3 How did I get myself here?

Reception

It is 5.30 in the evening and 'the lads', as the prison officers gathered in the reception area of Lancaster Farms Young Offenders Institution refer to them, are wondering when they will be called and checked in. Their faces are visible inside the glass-fronted kiosks where they wait. They have just piled out of an escort van delivering them from the courts; some have been convicted and given a prison sentence, others are on remand until the date of their next hearing.

Most are 18–21 years old, the older young offenders (YOs), although a few 15–17 year olds, the juveniles, have come through on the new Detention and Training Orders (DTOs). There is the odd gesture of strutting bravado, expressions intended to tell how untouched they are by the prospect of prison; some crack jokes, usually those who have served time before, whose parents have been inside or those for whom prison represents status – macho credentials. In this behaviour is mirrored the importance attached by those boys most likely to end up in prison to an image of toughness, to being seen as leaders of the pack by dint of what they say. This may mean letting the others know they understand the score and are in control, or it could be a remark that clearly contains the threat of violence to be directed against anyone who opposes them.

Juveniles may travel from court in the company of older YOs and they may be imprisoned in the same building, but they are separated at reception to conform with the new policy and kept in separate units to serve their sentences (see page 24). This is to protect juveniles from the potential risks posed by older, more experienced and possibly more brutalised YOs.

The newcomers who have not been in prison before, in many cases bewildered by what went on in court that day, look stunned and their faces seem to ask the question: how did I get myself here?

It is what Brendan, 15 and Tom Thumb tiny with a baby face and a conviction for arson that has put him away for a couple of years, says when I talk with him some months into his sentence. He has been out of school since primary level, drinking heavily by the time he was 12, taking drugs a year later. His childhood was spent 'running wild' – there is little sign that anyone bothered what he got up to. In his mind it was just 'more of the same' when he tried to set fire to the house of a girl who rejected him and he never thought about the consequences:

> 'I was completely out of it on Es and crack cocaine and a bit of drink too. It wasn't until I was arrested and questioned that I realised properly what I'd done. I hadn't burnt the place down and nobody was hurt. I didn't think they'd send me to prison, thought I was too young. But they did and I remember as they marched us through them big gates and I looked up at all the barbed wire and realised how serious it was I thought: "Oh Brendan, what did you do to get yourself here?"'

It was in reception that Lou, 16, in Holloway on a charge of selling stolen goods, recalls panicking:

> 'I had been so used to being free, knowing I could get out of anywhere and be on my own if I wanted, and here I was with NO freedom. The worst was thinking I couldn't just get into the outside air, see a mate. I'd just taken all that for granted even though I'd had the police on my case, been cautioned and all that shit.'

Prison ethnographer Anita Wilson spent several months studying young prisoners at a male YOI in the North and at a London female YOI observing children and young people. She summed up what she saw at reception:

> 'It is a place of vulnerability when most in-coming prisoners are still coming down from any combination of the shock of being sentenced, the trauma of the journey, the withdrawal from drugs, the panic of first time incarceration. It is a place which can change from being eerily quiet to bustling with activity in a matter of minutes depending upon the variable and sporadic influx of prisoners who need to be processed.'

Fear

Fear is the thing many of them talk about when describing arriving in prison. For the newcomers there was that incalculable fear of not knowing what could happen, of how it might happen. What was the worst they could expect? There is fear of officers and what they might do, but much stronger is the fear of other prisoners.

Prisoners are aware there may be some kind of initiation process as, indeed there was for Suliman, then 17, at Lancaster Farms:

> 'I was scared stiff when I first arrived with no idea what to expect. And my first night there were these other boys leaning out their windows yelling abuse at me ... dirty Paki and a lot worse. I knew if I just put up with it I'd be seen as weak so next morning I went up to the ring-leader and just had a go at him and we had a fight. I got into trouble for that and lost privileges but I had to prove I wasn't going to lie down and take it.'

So many of the young who end up in prison have grown up seeing life as a tough process, a world in which it's weak and foolish to trust other people, where they'll turn on you or let you down, given a chance. These are the feelings that can surface at reception:

Jimmy, 19, serving two years at Moorland, puts it like this:

> 'My parents taught me nobody was reliable. Either they loved me to bits or walloped me blue, they were sober one day, drunk as skunks the next until my Dad walked out and my Mum went mental. That was as frightening as it gets and it made me realise you don't depend on any-body to be safe. So when I came here that was how I saw it. Oh yes I felt scared but I knew I couldn't afford to. It was a question of showing you were top dog even if it meant fights and aggro. One thing you can't be seen as inside is a weakling – the Muppet.'

Do they all hate us?
The way officers greet new inmates has as big an impact as anything on how new arrivals feel about being in prison, and whether they will be able to cope.

Steve, 17, got off the bus at Portland to begin his sentence and, he recalls:

> 'There was this officer with his face in mine screaming: "We don't want any crap from you. If there's trouble you'll know about it." I was really, really scared. I'd heard what a harsh place this was and I wanted to work out how I could avoid getting into trouble and being done over or sent down to the punishment block.'

Billy, 16, remembers arriving at Aylesbury: 'This screw he just looked at me, really cold like, and said, "This is not a holiday camp, you are here because you're out of order, so now just get on with it." I remember think-ing then – do all the screws hate us?' By contrast Corinna, 16, was sur-prised when she arrived at Styal:

> 'I'd been toughening up inside, just trying not to feel anything, because I thought the screws would be really hard and cruel. I was dead fright-ened they were going to crutch me. But the officer who talked to me first was kind and she made me feel less scared. There are others like that who let you know they were there to help if you had problems.'

The officers meeting prisoners at this early stage often see tears, from the boys as well as the girls, although they do their best to disguise it. One officer checking in a youth in grimy track suit bottoms and a puffa jacket in cheap, shiny fabric who turns his head to the side and answers questions in cracked monosyllables, says afterwards:

> 'I can spot the ones who will be found later in their cells crying their hearts out, crying for their mothers. Oh I know some have done things you'd hate them for if you dwelt on it too much, and I can see they do need to be shown they can't go on that way. But all the same a lot of them seem so young and helpless once they are in here.'

Processing

At reception children are separated from older YOs, then prisoners are searched, an officer fills in their details and personal belongings are taken. They are given a prison number. There is a medical examination to ascer-tain if they are fit enough to be in prison and it is then that those consid-ered vulnerable and liable to self-harm – usually cutting themselves – or even to attempt suicide should be picked up. They are screened for drugs to see if detox is necessary.

It is a legal requirement that prisoners must be interviewed within 24 hours and given the information they need – the rules and requirements of the prison regime, their rights, who to turn to if they are being bullied or are in trouble.

How far the reception procedure can fulfil the Prison Service's aim of reducing anxiety and tension will depend to a great extent on how much time officers have available to talk with their new charges, to spot the vul-nerable and frightened and to go through what they may expect in a way that makes it clear. Prisons like Feltham where they receive a very large number of new arrivals – Feltham gets between 70 and 80 daily – may find it difficult to deal with the inmates as they would wish.

Janine Morris, as deputy governor of Feltham, was aware of how dam-aging is the fast-track and impersonal approach imposed on the reception staff by these huge numbers. She spoke about the situation:

'We know very well that youngsters arriving at reception need to be helped to cope with what is often a very traumatic experience. We need to be able to spot the vulnerable ones who may be a suicide risk, but how do you do that without adequate staff? The last near-suicide we had was a 15 year old who tried to harm himself on the first night in custody. Who knows, if he had been one of just 20 coming through, if we had had time to spot his fear and despair, he might not have tried to harm himself.'

At Lancaster Farms, too, officers expressed frustration at the speed with which they have to 'put through' the new arrivals; this at a prison where there is not the pressure of Feltham. But I was told repeatedly that they cannot afford to increase the number of officers for reception duties without having to make cuts to other parts of the regime. One officer voiced it this way:

'I've been working here for years and I know the kind of lives these kids have so often come from. At first I thought some of it couldn't be true, that they couldn't have had such tough childhoods, but you come to know it's all too true and that more than anything they need help. I'm a father and when I see a new batch of kids, scared out of their wits, with nothing in their lives to hang on to, I want to sit down with them for ten minutes, help them feel I'm someone they could trust, someone they can ask for if they want to later, as well as just writing their names on a sheet of paper and barking out the bits of information they need. But I can't do it. If I do the system breaks down. So far as I'm concerned it's yet another failure in these kids' lives.'

First impressions

It is not difficult to imagine the fear that prison buildings may instil in new arrivals. Steve arriving at Portland recalls the sick sinking feeling in his stomach: 'The building looked enormous and very scary. It's isolated, just standing there like a place where you will be locked away and never seen again. It was worse than I'd expected.'

Older YOs arriving at Moorland feel daunted by the building with its labyrinth of dimly lit corridors and, for all the landscaped gardens, the bleak stretch of landscape that seems to go on forever outside, the high fences and enormous iron gates.

James, 20, serving two years at this prison, says: 'I was 18 when I arrived and all the things I'd heard about what happens to young men in tough male jails came flooding into my mind. The building made it all so real. I could imagine us like wild animals trapped inside and with all sorts of brutality possible.'

David Lancaster, governor of Holloway with its network of dingy corridors and limited communal areas – it was designed as a psychiatric hospital in the 1970s – is the first to say the building is intimidating to new inmates. And although under his governorship the running of the YO unit has been commended, he would have liked a building designed for the juveniles they then housed there, which he felt would have done much to create a more caring atmosphere.

By contrast inmates arriving at Lancaster Farms, a custom-built prison in creamy stone with airy corridors and large, open association areas, have talked of finding it 'not as bad as I expected' when they arrived, in spite of the barbed wire and anti-roll bars along the fences. Styal too 'felt comforting – normal' in the word of one child imprisoned there for drug offences, because it is built as a series of houses with ordinary double rooms such as you might find in a small terraced house.

Jules, 17, arriving at Huntercombe, was amazed to see low-level buildings and to find far fewer barred doors and locks than he expected inside:

'But the thing that surprised me most was the kind of relaxed atmosphere and there were inmates calling some staff by their Christian name. That blew my mind. In a way it was confusing, it didn't make sense. Was this or wasn't it prison? And were they playing some devious mind games by making it look this way? That was what I wondered at first, but I soon learned that my first impression was right: it's a place where they want you not to feel scared and obsessed with the fact you are in prison.'

The induction programme

All young offenders are given a mandatory induction programme lasting one week or longer. However because the juvenile regime is different from that for older YOs a different approach is taken. In guidelines for the treatment of juveniles the government has defined the objective as: 'To identify, assess and record the needs, abilities and aptitudes of every individual and draw up a sentence plan with them.' For juveniles on a DTO the planning will include provision for that part of their time to be served outside. But there is far less focus on the needs of older YOs than on those of the 15–17 year olds, even though many of the older prisoners are as immature and in need of care and support as the juveniles.

Although the induction week is meant to cover basic things to do with understanding how the prison works, standards of behaviour, how to cope with difficult situations, the anti-bullying ethos, education, drugs and health, it is widely agreed by many people I spoke to, from reformers to governors, officers to inmates, that the quantity and quality of what goes on in this induction week varies greatly.

Steive Butler coordinates induction programmes at Huntercombe where they include role play and dynamic group activities intended to get newcomers to think about some of the issues that have landed them inside and may affect how they get on. But this is certainly not done in all YOIs.

A number of prisoners spoke of finding the induction programme helpful. Suzie, 18, at Holloway is one:

> 'My Mum had been in prison and she told me what she knew, but that was frightening and I thought I'd be shut up a lot and that everything would be very hard. At induction they talked to us like we were kids and explained what would happen in a day, how the point of prison was to help us do something with our lives. And they made a big thing about bullying not being tolerated. I felt better after that, like there were people who actually cared about us.'

Billy, 18, addicted to heroin and homeless when he was sent to Moorland for theft, was less impressed:

> 'A lot of mouthwash as far as I was concerned. The prison nobs talking like it was so easy to get your life together and then go out there and get work and live a good citizen's life. Well I know it's not like that and they can teach me bricklaying and computer skills till the cows come home and bloody take off again, but who's going to take me on with a record like mine when they can choose from other people who are clean? I know I disappointed them with my attitude from the start, but it's their fault being so full of hope … like f****** Father Christmas wanting to be thanked for making life happy.'

Prison ethnographer Anita Wilson, who spent time working at Lancaster Farms, saw how quickly prisoners changed and adapted in significant ways from the first 'viewing' in reception. The induction programme was an important part of their becoming socialised into prison life:

> 'By this stage prisoners have already begun to be integrated into the prison regime. Unlock, lock-down, meal-times, exercise and association times fall in line with the timetabling of the rest of the jail. The prisoner will have learned where and if he is allowed to smoke, where he can watch communal TV, who to be aware of. He will probably have made some attempt to retain links with his outside world and to initiate some social networks among fellow prisoners.'

Induction is also a way of getting inmates to face up to the fact that they have been found guilty and need to accept this, says Paul McDowell, new deputy governor at Feltham. Several governors have commented on how particularly the young prisoners huff and puff for the first week or weeks, insisting they were wrongly convicted, will soon be out on appeal and will 'show them' they are innocent once out.

Several governors spoke of how important it was to make contact with new prisoners, ideally during their induction time. Paul Mainwaring while at Huntercombe invited each one in to see him individually:

> 'I ask them what their interests are, what they are good at, a bit about themselves and how they feel they can best spend their time with us. I don't dwell on their crime. They've been punished for that by the courts and our job here is to help them use their time constructively and be in a position to make the choice not to reoffend if that's what they want. I think getting the relationship straight and making inmates feel valued from the beginning is critical.'

Personal officers

During induction prisoners are assigned a personal officer who is supposed to take a particular interest in them and, ideally, acts as an informal mentor. These personal officers can at best be a significant adult for the young person, providing a role model, parental-style guidance and support when they are in difficulties. They may help their charge to learn to live within the boundaries of the prison and demonstrate that it can be safe to trust an adult. At best, in the view of Robbie at Huntercombe, you get the kind of help he did:

> 'I was given a young woman personal officer I got on with straight away. She really seemed to want to know all about me from the start – not something I was used to – and she worked hard to get me opportunities, and to help me when I was down. She was really important in helping me not get out of control like I had been in the past when I just felt disliked by everyone in the prisons I was sent to.'

At Styal several girls talked of how they had been treated with unexpected kindness by the officers assigned to them. Gemma, 16, relates:

> 'I was so angry when I arrived and I just "knew" everyone would hate me. I had decided I'd shut off from the screws because they were the ones imprisoning me. So when this screw says she's my personal officer I was just "oh yeah?" But she was really quiet and easy and just said she was there if I wanted her but she wouldn't bother me except to tell me the things I had to know. That took me by surprise because I expected

her to start ordering me about. After that she would come in and see me in the cell and just chat a bit. I started liking her and telling her things. In the end I was telling her everything about my rotten, stinking life.'

It is, however, widely acknowledged that the personal officer scheme is very patchy, partly because some officers are not interested in taking this role with prisoners whom they may see as a 'bad lot' and in need of being taught a lesson – an attitude I heard expressed on more than one occasion.

That was the experience of Joe, 19, at Moorland:

'This screw, he tells me he's my personal officer and that I'm to tell him if there's any problems and that. But you know what, he was a bastard. He was always telling me off, shouting at me and I got the feeling he said bad things about me to them in charge. There's no way I'd have told him of my problems or asked him to help because I think he'd have used it to make a fool of me.'

Then there are personal officers who would like to take on a caring role, but as it is a duty they must perform on top of their usual tasks as officer on the wing, and often for several prisoners, this ambition may well be thwarted. A woman officer at a male YOI she did not want named described the dilemma:

'I'm responsible for six lads and I feel they all need daily attention. But the other day the fiancée of one of them died and he was, quite naturally, very upset. I arranged for him to speak to his parents and have a special visit but it took extra time and so my other kids were short-changed. If that happens a lot it can be quite damaging to the relationships you try to build up.'

Getting to know the officers

For new prisoners there is the challenge of getting to know all the staff and how to spot 'the screws from the officers' as Michelle, 17, in the Holloway juvenile unit put it:

'The screws are the ones who make it plain they are doing a job and they're not interested in you. In fact they quite often go out of their way to be mean or hard and unkind. There are quite a few around like that. But officers are the okay ones, and some are really kind. There's an officer I always ask to speak to if I've had a row here or got a bad letter or some other problem's come up. She's not my personal officer but just the same she does what she can for me.'

There was a touching affection at Styal among many of the girls for

Lorraine Holt, a former senior officer who clearly took a maternal rather than authoritarian approach. She had worked with them for a number of years and knew well the neediness many have:

> 'Too many have never known any affection, they don't know what good emotions feel like. They talk a lot about being empty and numb inside and they use drugs and drink to try to get rid of these sensations, but in the end they make it worse and of course so often it's drugs and drink that lead them into crime. Then it's our job to try to get them into a better state. I do wonder when I hear what some have been through how they can be rehabilitated, but if you stick at it and are consistent they do get to trust you.'

In the younger boys you see a child-like desire to find a big brother or father figure and a number find one or two officers whom they put into that role. But conversely they feel a particular hostility towards those they see as rejecting them – in the way so many have been rejected in life outside. Among staff who clearly feel involved with their young charges and who take seriously the belief that they can make a difference there is acceptance of this attitude:

> 'If we have to be a bit firm with lads in the beginning we're known as screws – it's a stereotype and a defence against the fear many of the lads feel. But if we treat them fairly and decently they usually come to the point where they feel they can talk to you.'

Robbie, who recognises how antagonistic he was towards the world after leaving care and finding himself without friends or support, knows he played his part in setting officers against him in the prisons he went to before Huntercombe :

> 'I would take the piss, wind officers up and be mouthy and I guess I saw the worst of screw behaviour. There is a pathetic argument among the screws which is that it's their job to punish baddies – nothing else, just to be Mr I'll-show-you-how-tough-life-is. They do things like putting you into your cell for 23½ hours with absolutely nothing in it. It's terrible but it makes you stronger and more angry with authority.'

He describes too the contrast with how it was at Huntercombe while he was there:

> 'On the whole they behave in a friendly way and particularly Steive Butler who is brilliant. She's given me such opportunities. If I make it on the outside I'll have her to thank a lot because she got me a college

place, organised for me to produce the prison magazine with desktop publishing because I'm very keen on computers. It's ironic that you have to go to prison to find someone who cares that much.'

By contrast Sharon, 17, at Holloway would not let her guard down with any officer:

'They can be all nice to you one day then really bad and bitchy the next for no reason. Some of the girls here imagine screws are really their friends but that's bollocks. They haven't chosen us, we're dumped on them and they've a job to do. Why should they care about us? Of course they don't so I'm not going to care about them.'

Chris Tchaikovsky, an ex-prisoner who set up the campaigning organisation Women in Prison, acknowledges that there are some officers who are genuinely concerned with the welfare and happiness of their charges and go out of their way to show it, but she also warns that there is a limit on how close they can get to an inmate:

'It is simply not possible for prisoners to let their guard down and confide in officers or trust them completely because in the end they have to represent authority. Take this situation: one minute an officer is comforting a woman who is missing her child or who has heard of a death in the family, then the next minute if rules say it's time she has to slam the door on that inmate and turn the key in the lock.'

The way prison officers behave is absolutely critical to the way prison functions, which is why Paul McDowell, deputy governor at Feltham, is willing to criticise what he sees as bad practice:

'Things are made very difficult at Feltham because the staff culture here is delinquent. That doesn't mean all officers are behaving this way and in fact a great many are absolutely fine, but there is a significant minority who think that all the decisions we take should be about making their lives easier rather than prisoners' lives better.'

The personal views of officers greatly affect whether the prison regime is seen as being about rehabilitation with the idea that the inmates should be helped to make something of their lives, or whether it is seen as simply being about incarceration in a punitive regime with no particular interest in the end product. At best officers can create an atmosphere of justice, respect and humanity – something several prisoners at Huntercombe described even though they had all, at times, been punished for 'causing trouble'. But in several of the prisons visited governors and their deputies talked despairingly about the grip that the Prison Officers' Association (POA) had, and, it seemed, felt powerless to deal with this. When the POA formed, in the words of one governor, 'a bloody-minded cabal deciding amongst themselves how things would be', it could be very difficult to institute the changes they desired. Soon after I visited Feltham, Sir David Ramsbotham came out with a damning criticism of the POA there.

Cells

During the induction week prisoners stay in cells on the induction block, so it is not until they move on to the main wing that they see the places where they will sleep and spend a good deal of time. In the first days prisoners may smash up their cells regardless of whether these are reasonable or appalling. As one officer described: 'We see a lot of smashing up, kicking off because these kids can't accept they've got themselves into this mess and they're angry. Angry with themselves but they blame prison as though we asked them to come here.'

Later, when they move on to the main wing, cells assume a particular importance particularly if inmates are locked up for a long time. While it is now obligatory for juveniles to be out for a full day of activities – although it does not always happen – there is no such requirement for the older YOs, and they may languish for many hours of the day behind a locked door if there are insufficient officers to get them out or not enough activities available for them.

The way inmates regard their cells varies considerably. This depends partly on whether their cell is a cramped, battered-looking place with a lidless lavatory in the corner and nothing that represents comfort, or whether they are in modern, reasonably spacious cells. At worst, prisoners may find themselves in cells where there are offensive graffiti on the walls, racist slogans and swastikas.

The kind of cell prisoners are allocated on the main prison block will depend on behaviour. There are three levels of cell – basic, which are the bleakest and least hospitable; prisoners who lose good behaviour points can be sent here. Standard cells are where they start off and will stay unless their behaviour is sufficiently good for them to be rewarded by being put on the enhanced regime with better cells. The enhanced cells, where I visited an inmate at Moorland, were clean, relatively comfortable and opened onto a light, freshly painted landing.

Mixing in cells

Worryingly, although juvenile and older prisoners are now separated as a safety precaution, the same care is not necessarily taken when mixing different kinds of offenders in the same age-group. When prisoners are put in cells together regardless of attitudes or mental condition, things can go

50

badly wrong. Several prisoners talked of sharing a cell with inmates who frightened, bullied or intimidated them and of finding it hard to get officers to take this seriously. At worst there may be the kind of incident – although it must be said this is rare – where an inmate is seriously injured or killed by their cellmate. This happened at Feltham in March 2000 when a young Asian, Zahid Mubarek, in for a very minor offence, was killed the night before he was due for release by his cellmate, who was known to have a severe personality disorder as well as racist attitudes.

Children and young people who have committed minor, non-violent offences may also find themselves in cells with prisoners in for far more serious, dangerous and sophisticated offences and who may well influence them. The 'academy for crime' situation is all too real. Young prisoners told me how much they had learned that would help them commit a wider range of crimes than they had considered before and to carry them out more effectively. No less worrying were the number who said they had learned to be tough and hard in a way they hadn't contemplated before. Several said they had begun to think about carrying a knife if, on the outside, they went into crime again.

Mihash, 20, who has been in prison on and off since he was 16, is a prime example:

'First time I was put inside I was a babe. I'd stolen from warehouses, breaking in at night through locks, and I'd done some shoplifting, but I really couldn't have coped with anything bigger or more scary. Inside I learnt about all the ways you can get into a locked house, how to produce a knife to frighten someone into doing what you want. And there were lads talking about rapes they'd done, how you overpower a woman. I've never done that but if I wanted to I'd be better equipped since my education in prison.'

Tough guys

In a tough-guy macho culture it is no surprise that there is a competitive boastfulness with young inmates vying to tell the biggest, boldest story of their crimes. Steive Butler at Huntercombe hears a lot of it and particularly amongst the youngest inmates:

'They're so bolshie about getting caught, saying it won't happen next time, how they're going to do this that and whatever .... They talk like they're going to be the big-time glamorous criminals with homes abroad, big cars, flashy wives, non-stop clubbing and champagne and you just know they'll get caught the very next time they try some small-time crime because they don't really have a clue how to live properly, let alone plan sophisticated crimes.'

'When children and young people are put on remand they experience all the negative impact of prison as a sentenced offender. They are traumatised and disadvantaged, they are taken out of school, if they are attending, and it can be hard to get them back in. Work, if they have it, may be lost, and family life is frequently disrupted. And at the end of it all there's a good chance they will not even be found guilty.'

Mark Ashford, defence lawyer

4 Remanded in custody

'Remand was bad. I was that frightened what was going to happen to me because you hear stories outside about what goes on inside ... but I wasn't even part of the prison. I didn't belong and I didn't trust the screws. I was in a cell with someone I wouldn't have walked on the same street as outside and he did my head in with all his mad talk about what "they" would do to us. I was in my cell almost all the time, even eating meals, and all I did was worry about what was going on outside with my family and my girlfriend. The joke is I felt better when I was given a prison sentence because then I knew what was going on, what I had to do and it was just a question of getting through the time.'
Tony, 19, serving a sentence at Moorland.

Remand is limbo time, a waiting game, a seemingly limitless sentence to unsentenced time. The frightened, disoriented memories of those I spoke with echoed the findings of Ken Smith, writer-in-residence at Wormwood Scrubs in 1985: 'Prisoners years on in the system remember this first impact of prison vividly. Remand *is* worse, the old hands say, meaning worse than the lot of the convicted. Remands are crowded and packed in together among too many unknown quantities.'[1]

For many young people, then, remand in custody is the harshest and most frightening time they spend in prison. Remands in custody are made either when a defendant is awaiting trial or after they have been convicted and the court is waiting for reports on their background and mental state before passing sentence. You might presume that those who have not been found guilty would be given the best treatment possible but in fact the opposite is all too often true. Children and young people remanded to prison frequently receive worse treatment than their convicted peers; it is a time when mental health problems can become acute and frightened young people are likely to harm themselves. It is a situation that angered Sir David Ramsbotham during his time as Chief Inspector of Prisons: 'No mention is made anywhere [in the Prison Service's Statement of Purpose] of those not yet sentenced, who in the eyes of the law, are presumed innocent until proved guilty, and therefore should, in logic, receive better treatment and conditions than those in custody.'

So it is particularly shocking that juveniles, those whom it is most imperative to keep out of prison, are increasingly being locked up on remand. During 1995, 1,626 boys aged 15–17 years were remanded in custody (398 untried); in 2000 the number had risen to 2,345 (359 untried). For girls of the same age the situation is still more dramatic. During 1995, 49 were locked up on remand (11 untried); in 2000 the number was 89 (13 untried) – almost double. There has been a small drop in the overall number of boys and young men (14–20 years) remanded in custody, from 2,701 to 2,481, suggesting that older boys are being given bail more often. But the opposite is true of girls and young women, where the total figure of 14–20 year olds has risen from 88 in 1995 to 126 in 2000.[2]

Notwithstanding the fact that remand in custody can be profoundly damaging in practical, emotional and psychological ways, organisations such as the Howard League and Nacro estimate that some 50% of under-21 year olds who are remanded do not then receive custodial sentences. This would tie in with statistics for the total prison population which, in 1999, show that almost a quarter of remanded prisoners were acquitted or their cases not proceeded with, and nearly 26% were given non-custodial sentences or discharged.[3]

Policy and practice

Any person in criminal proceedings has a right to bail, but in certain circumstances the courts can refuse this – for example if the juvenile or young person is charged with a very serious offence such as murder, attempted murder, manslaughter, rape or attempted rape. Bail may also be refused if the defendant has been in breach of bail conditions in the past or if the court is satisfied there are substantial grounds for believing the defendant would abscond if given bail, that they would commit an offence while on bail or interfere with witnesses or obstruct the course of justice in other ways.[4]

A decade ago the Criminal Justice Act 1991, passed by the Conservative government, abolished remand into prison custody for all children under 17 years – over-17 year olds are defined as adults for remand purposes. To replace this the government introduced a Security Requirement which meant the courts had the power to remand 15 and 16 year olds directly to secure accommodation if they thought that it was necessary to protect the public from them, or that they would harm themselves. But because there were not enough secure unit places at the time, provision was made for 15 and 16 year old boys to be placed in prison custody until enough secure unit places were created. In theory it is illegal for girls of this age to be sent to prison on remand – although some still are for the same reason.

Successive UK governments have evidently placed little value on the United Nations Standard Minimum Rules for the Administration of Juvenile Justice (1985),[5] by which the UK is bound, which state very clearly that detention of unconvicted children should only ever be used as a last resort and for the shortest possible time. There are currently about 450 places available in local authority secure units, considerably fewer than needed. An added pressure on places came when the Crime and Disorder Act 1998 gave courts the power to put 12–14 year olds of both sexes into secure units or secure training centres if they wanted to give them a custodial remand. This means, according to the Children's Society, that there are now even fewer places for 15–16 year old boys and so they continue to be remanded into prison. The courts are recommended to remand a 15–16 year old boy to local authority secure accommodation only if he is deemed emotionally vulnerable, immature and likely to self-harm, but even then if there are no places available this may not happen, as is surely clear from the self-harm and suicides that occur on juvenile remand wings.

The amount of time children and young people spend on remand, whether in a prison or in a secure unit, will depend on the type of crime. Once bail is refused a time limit is set for the next hearing: this is either 56 days from the first appearance to summary trial in a magistrates court or 70 days from the first appearance to committal to the crown court. The maximum time spent on remand should therefore be 8–10 weeks. However, the prosecution can apply for time limits to be extended if they can convince the court that they need more time for evidence to be gathered, which means young defendants may spend months or even longer on remand. The Children's Society cites cases where a young person has been held on remand for a year pending trial and sentence. But if no time extension is given and the limit runs out then the defendant must be given bail.

One of the most serious complaints made has always been that young remands do not have access to facilities and a regime in the same way as sentenced prisoners. With the introduction of the juvenile estate of 15–17 year olds, including those on remand, prisons were set national standards for their regime and education. However, no such standards apply for the older defendants on remand, and although they may be offered the opportunity to join in prison activities, this will not necessarily happen. Particularly unfair, if you consider how close the needs of a young adult just turned 18 are to those of juveniles, is that they effectively 'pay' for the implementation of the new juvenile estate. Prison staff explain that the legal requirement to meet the standards of the juvenile estate regime even for children on remand often means there is not enough time available for older remands at sports facilities, for example – in one YOI there was just one 'dawn chorus' hour free first thing in the morning. Nor may there be staff available to accompany older remands to activities or teachers to deliver education for them. All too often too much of this limbo time is spent 'banged up' in their cells.

Prisons like Feltham, which receive a very high number of new remand prisoners every day, may be able to do little more for inmates on Feltham B wing (where the 18–21 year olds are held) than process them, find them cells, attend to their most basic needs, and prepare them for their court appearances. And without proper resourcing for remand prisoners they are likely to continue to get, in the words of one officer, 'the scrag end' of treatment.

In these constrained conditions remanded prisoners have none of the distractions or chance of making social contacts that convicted prisoners have. Jimmy, 19, who went on to serve a sentence for ABH, shudders remembering his time on remand:

'I felt like a creature kept in a cage, I spent that long inside that cell. It freaked me after a while, thought I was going mad because I'd worked on building sites and I was used to air and space and using my body and having mates around. I didn't have anyone I'd call anything like a mate during that time. My cellmate's head was being done in just the same so we weren't much help to each other.'

These unconvicted inmates are isolated from a place in prison society and the camaraderie and united front against authority which is a way in which young prisoners bond and which can be an important psychological mediator of the fear and uncertainty they feel inside. It is not difficult to imagine the pressure-cooker emotions of a young person who arrives frightened and confused after their time in court, not knowing what to expect, and young defendants will often have heard that remand is the toughest and nastiest time and so will be very anxious about what may happen. Rocky, 18, on remand in Feltham, describes the experience:

'Remand prisoners deal with their fears by frightening newer remands. Some of the ones who have been through the process before act very macho. So there's a lot of talk about the worst prisons and how the new remands might get sent to a really bad one. You are told endless stories of horror experiences and that's when you don't have a clue if you might get one year or five if you are found guilty. I just hope the courts will believe I am innocent, that's how I keep going, but I've seen other guys crack.'

Young people on remand may also be coming down off drink and drugs and, in the case of girls and young women especially, they may be on medication for depression which is interrupted or even stopped. And although sentenced and unsentenced juveniles must be accommodated in a separate unit, there is nothing to stop them or older remands, who may be committing very unsophisticated crimes, being put in with prisoners who are established offenders happy to 'educate' someone who has just entered the criminal justice system. Or they may be put in with someone who bullies or frightens them.

Not surprisingly, given the pressures and uncertainty, rates of mental health problems are perceived to be markedly higher among remands than among sentenced YOs. The most powerful indicator of the distress and mental instability young people on remand experience is that they are substantially more likely to kill themselves than those who are serving a sentence in prison. In the decade between 1990–2001 there were 56 self-inflicted deaths by 15–21 year olds on remand in prison in England and Wales compared with 87 suicides by convicted YOs, although the latter population over the decade was about six times larger than the remand population.[6]

The father of Sam, who killed his mother during a psychotic episode, recalls visiting his son who was on remand at North Allerton YOI, 'a very cold, old, damp prison':

> 'He told me he was very scared. He cried himself to sleep each night and there was nobody to help him deal with his distress which he told me was unbearable. It took a long time for him to go through remand so he did make friends but they were all people like himself and they couldn't help him. The staff were good there and they recognised he was at risk – in fact he tried to kill himself five times and several other youngsters tried too, only you never hear about all the attempts – but there were too few staff and resources. It was really only when Sam was put on the hospital wing that there were people with time to care for him.'

All the governors I met agreed that they would like to do better by their remand prisoners but had no resources to make improvements. Even so some prisons do endeavour to put older remands onto at least a partial regime. And at Holloway, governor David Lancaster told me very emphatically that all their remands had the same regime as convicted prisoners.

The injustice and undesirability of remanding young defendants who are not classified as a risk seems obvious, yet, according to lawyer Mark Ashford, remand is still used by some magistrates for relatively minor alleged law-breaking, such as driving offences. Ashford has also heard a magistrate giving an unconvicted young defendant a custodial remand 'to teach him a lesson'. In a 1995 survey of 15 year old boys on remand in Feltham, the vast majority were found to be there for alleged property crime, usually burglary.[7]

Alternatives to custodial remand

For campaigning organisations, and defence lawyers like Ashford, providing bail support schemes as an alternative to remand is a priority. The way bail support works is that the advocate for the child or young person organises some kind of care placement, foster home, or other supportive placement designed to convince the courts that the young defendant can safely be given bail. Larry Wright, YOT manager at Hammersmith and Fulham, explains how it worked for a juvenile in one case:

'There was a young boy who robbed a woman tourist of her personal jewellery – a serious offence which would have virtually guaranteed a remand in custody even though he was very contrite. He was remanded but we managed to set up a situation that convinced the courts they could let him out on bail. He had accommodation and the arrangement was that he should spend time with us five days a week. He complied with this and really established a productive relationship. He very willingly did offence-focused work and group work with other young defendants. He also got a job.

'It would have been impossible to work like this with him in prison and what it meant was that, when we went back to court, we could tell them how well he had done. The result was he got two years supervision with a 90-day community sentence. But if he had been on remand in prison I'm certain he'd have got a custodial sentence.'

This echoes the experience of Ashford who relates how he managed to find remand foster parents for a young defendant, who drew up a very structured programme for his time and gave him regular meals and clean clothes – things he was not used to. Ashford recalls:

'Because he was eating and sleeping properly he calmed down and I was able to get him to focus on what was happening, he was there for our meetings and was able to concentrate so we could prepare his case properly. The day he was due in court his foster mother made sure he looked clean, tidy and well dressed which made a good impression. He spoke well and he was given a non-custodial sentence. My guess is if he had been remanded in custody he would have been in a state when he got into court and unable to explain himself properly.'

In 1997 the Children's Society took over the work the Howard League for Penal Reform had been doing in 'rescuing' children who had been remanded in custody by similarly offering the courts acceptable alternatives. The Society goes into prisons and secure units and attempts to obtain release for children aged 12–17 years. Between December 1999 and November 2000 it succeeded in getting 392 children removed from prison, some into secure units and 294 onto bail or bail support schemes. Sharon Moore, who set up this Remand Review initiative, explains:

> 'We speak to the young person, the parent, the solicitor and the Youth Offending Team worker. We then try to agree a planned approach to the case so that wherever possible a child can be released back into the community with support. This might mean for instance finding foster care for the bail period. Or if this is not possible we aim to have them transferred to a secure unit.'

The shocking rise in the number of 15–17 year olds remanded in custody (page 53) demonstrates how little the courts understand how profoundly damaging this time inside can be and the risks it poses to the mental well-being of young people awaiting trial. Remands are not in prison to be punished and yet they may actually suffer more than convicted prisoners. As the Children's Society demonstrates with its remand work, it is possible to find satisfactory and workable alternatives to remand and this is something that YOTs and the courts need to address. The scale of remand for children and young people is a great injustice, particularly when about half will be released when a verdict is reached.

NOTES

1. Ken Smith, *Inside Time*. London, Harrap, 1989.
2. *Prison Statistics, England and Wales*. London, Home Office, 1995–2000.
3. *Prison Statistics, England and Wales*. London, Home Office, 1999.
4. Mark Ashford and Alex Chard, *Defending Young People*. London, Legal Action Group, 2000.
5. The United Nations Standard Minimum Rules for the Administration of Juvenile Justice (The Beijing Rules), 1985, Nos. 13.1 and 13.2, state: 'Detention pending trial shall be used only as a measure of last resort and for the shortest possible time. Wherever possible [it] shall be replaced by alternative measures, such as close supervision, intensive care or placement with a family or in an educational setting or home.'
6. *Deaths in Prison 1990–2001 (England and Wales)*, Statistical Information. London, Inquest, 2001; *Prison Statistics, England and Wales*. London, Home Office, 2000.
7. *Troubleshooter: A project to rescue 15 year olds from prison*. London, Howard League for Penal Reform, 1995.

'They are in prison in a world apart with its own savage style, its own manners, its own lingo, invisible to the rest of us.'

Ken Smith, former prison writer-in-residence and author of *Inside Time* (London, Harrap, 1989)

5 *Wholly unacceptable*

Glen, 19, displays his tattooed arms conspicuously, and his voice has a don't-mess-with-me tone. He is in prison for the third time, serving three years for violence against the person, and he talks about how time inside has taught him that nobody will look after him and being hard is the best way in life.

'My first time inside I was sent to Feltham. It was a battlefield. There is a lot of testosterone flying around and there is a pecking order. You have to get your place in it or you will go under. They had this brilliant idea that if they put a bunch of offenders together they will get on nicely and sing songs. In fact it is a quick way of dividing the weak from the strong. The weak get bullied in front of everyone for the enjoyment of the strong and nobody takes much notice. The point is it doesn't matter to the officers if we mangle each other. Why should it? We're not their kids.'

Naim, a 21 year old Asian man who had almost completed two years for aggravated burglary at Moorland Young Offender Institution when we met, was resigned to being locked up and 'having to get through my time' when he was first sent there. What he had not anticipated was entering his cell and finding the words BNP and Combat 18 scribbled on the walls along with what the author would like to do with 'dirty Pakis and blacks'. Then there was the chipped paintwork and the general sense of decay in the cell. He never got used to using the in-cell lavatory knowing his cellmate could hear and smell everything.

What should punishment be?

When young people are sent to prison convicted of crimes, do we see loss of liberty as their punishment or do we regard what happens to them there as also part of the punishment? How far is there tacit acceptance that the young who offend against society deserve what they get? It is important that we consider these things for they raise fundamental questions about how far aspects of prison life that are degrading and humiliating, or that form a part of prison subculture rather than the official regime, should be tolerated.

When Sir David Ramsbotham, former HM Chief Inspector of Prisons, inspected Portland YOI at the end of the 1990s he came away inveighing against 'wholly unacceptable treatment and conditions for young offenders, including children'.[1] He made similar judgements on other YOIs that he and his team inspected. But once the doors are locked on the children and young adults whom the courts decide to remove from society it is all too easy to wipe from our minds what goes on in their daily lives – the 'hidden agenda of banged up' as one inmate described it.

In this chapter I have drawn together the aspects of prison life that prisoners are very often powerless to control or deal with and that are not, ostensibly, intended to be part of the punishment prescribed by the law. Among these are racism, bullying and mental health problems, exacerbated by the prison environment. The section on self-harm and suicide looks at how young people who feel they cannot cope with life inside may choose these self-destructive options. It is these 'unofficial' aspects of prison life that frequently cause the most distress and despair as well as volatile emotions, anger and a furious desire to get back at someone – anyone. All of this disrupts regimes, routines and prison welfare.

Race

In June 2000, of the 8,530 15–21 year olds in custody in England and Wales 81% were white, 13.2% black, 2.8% Asian and 3% Chinese, as compared with 92.4% white, 2.4% black, 4.1% Asian and 0.3% Chinese in the general population (all ages) of England and Wales in 2000.[2]

There is no evidence to suggest that people from ethnic minority groups commit proportionately more offences than white people. Indeed self-report studies, which are considered by many to be a more accurate measure of crime rates than the number who get caught by the police, showed a one per cent higher number of whites reporting that they had committed crimes than blacks, while the number of Asians was markedly lower.[3]

This is something Jamie, 19, who is white and serving time at Lancaster Farms, believes to be true:

'Lots of people think of blacks as the worst criminals because they are on the streets so much, and because when people think of crime they think "muggers" and then they think "black". But you know where I come from there's lots of black and Asian kids and they are my friends so I see how they get hassle and picked up when we white kids are overlooked for the same things.'

Robson, 18, feels blacks like himself can be pushed into a situation where they offend: 'If you're black there's all that stuff with the police on your case the whole time, thinking you've done wrong when you haven't. Sometimes you lose your rag and then they get you for that.'

Yet the high rate of stopping and arresting of black and Asian youth docs not mean that ethnic minorities are more likely to be found guilty of crimes than young whites are. In fact among those accused, ethnic minority defendants are more likely than whites to have their cases terminated early before court proceedings; in magistrates' courts the acquittal rate in contested trials is higher for black and Asian defendants than for white defendants; and ethnic minority defendants are less likely than whites to be convicted.[4] In other words, the inequality that ethnic minorities, and especially black young people, experience takes the form of their having a greater chance than young whites of being put through the criminal justice system and of being charged, yet ultimately being less likely to end up with a conviction. However, they are both more likely to be remanded in custody than whites, and to get longer sentences when they are convicted, and hence they are 'over-represented' in prison.[5]

This is something that Mark Ashford, who specialises in defending young people at risk of suffering discrimination because of colour, class or social disadvantage, has observed: 'Right through the criminal system if they are black they are looked down on and to a lesser extent that applies to other ethnic minorities. The prejudice is fantastic.'

Racism in prison

Lee, 18, serving a year for robbery at Moorland, feels that being black means he gets more punishment than his white peers:

'In here I've got racism coming at me from all sides from inmates and officers. You are seen as different from day one and you have to put up with racist name-calling and insults and then if you complain to the officers, some at least, they act like you're getting above yourself or else you are treated like you are lying. The whites don't get that. Oh sure bad things happen to them and some are given plenty of grief by the bigger guys, but that happens to us as well as the racist stuff.'

A commitment to tackle the problems of racism experienced by prisoners was made by Martin Narey, Director General of the Prison Service, as we entered the new millennium with the publication of the Prison Service document *Respond*. This contained a set of objectives intended to confront racial harassment and discrimination in prison and to make sure something was done about it even though, Martin Narey insisted, the Prison Service was already 'proactive' in tackling racism on behalf of prisoners.

Feltham, which receives prisoners from the Greater London area, generally has more black inmates than white, yet the importance attached to learning how best to tackle racism can be gauged by the fact that a number of officers talked to me of not having been to anti-racism meetings for two years. They put it down to staff shortages, saying that they had to choose between taking inmates to activities or attending the meetings and decided the former was more important. The way they expressed this left the impression that they did not rate 'race awareness-raising' sessions very highly.

John Harding, speaking as head of the Inner London Probation Service before he retired in 2001, wondered whether Narey knew what his commitment actually meant on a day-to-day basis because:

'Fifty per cent of the young people we get involved with are black and we hear of them having terrible experiences. Places like Portland YOI have, traditionally been riddled with racism. We have gone there and challenged those in charge about racism. It's no place to send a young black kid. The majority of the staff are white and they do not understand the diversity or cultural difference at all. So what chance is there of staff taking prisoner racism seriously in those circumstances?'

Many black prisoners I spoke with said they had not noticed much being done to combat racism during the 'proactive' years before the *Respond* document emerged.

The thing that rankles for Jason, 18, serving a sentence at Moorland for aggravated burglary, is a sense of betrayal:

'When I came a lot was made of how there's a black support group and the staff are really keen on it. Then I went into the room where the staff do crosswords and saw this bit of paper. On the back there was the word black. Someone had crossed it out and put "wog" instead. That was a member of the support group who done it so how can you trust people like that?'

The *Respond* document stressed the importance of an accessible and efficient complaints procedure for prisoners, with all complaints being logged and reported to the Home Office. There is, however, is a good deal of scepticism among prisoners about how well this scheme can work. A view expressed to me in two YOIs when I was discussing how ethnic minority prisoners deal with racism was: 'We can fill in forms all day long but what guarantee have we got they'll ever be logged and sent on? These officers can say what they like to you to cover their backs, and what can we do?'

On the other hand, Luke, 18, at Moorland, who felt one officer in particular did not like him, was reassured when it seemed his complaint had been reported:

> 'I had been given a really bad time by this dude who really disliked blacks. He certainly didn't like me. I told this other officer who was safe, really good to me he was, and he immediately said it would be reported. I don't know what happened after that but I didn't get more hassle.'

Officers who may be careful to avoid racist talk or behaviour so that they cannot be identified as racists themselves may nevertheless be seen by inmates as ignoring racist abuse by white prisoners on other prisoners. But Marcus, a 20 year old Afro-Caribbean in Feltham, took a different view based on several months in custody: 'These officers may not even like black people but then they have a good way of separating personal and political beliefs from their work ... and some do intervene if a white talks bad to a black. I've been in Aylesbury where it was very different and much worse.'

YOIs must now have an anti-racist policy and amongst those I visited all had their mission statements prominently pasted up. This did not impress Donovan, a lanky 19 year old Afro-Caribbean lad sentenced to 18 months at Moorland who says intention is one thing, willingness to implement it by staff another: 'Some officers are safe and respect you, but that anti-racist statement don't mean toss all to those screws who don't like black people and think we're all like bad. I've had an officer who has taken against me coming right up close and saying, "you nigger you".'

Racism among prisoners

Several prisoners from ethnic minority backgrounds voiced the view expressed by Jack, 17, a London teenager of African descent who has been in prison three times and is now at Lancaster Farms, that you had to expect 'racist shit' when you went to prison.

> 'You just know you're going to have to put up with racism. You can't go into prison and get treated same as whites because they don't think you are the same. When I was on the induction wing of one YOI I was subjected to racist abuse non-stop – shouting out the windows, attacks when I went to the shower, this and that.'

Jack was one of several prisoners with stories of how staff attitudes affect the extent to which inmates can get away with racism: 'I complained next day and the officer said it was the New Year and that I should "leave it out". Her words exactly.'

If racial discrimination on the outside makes life hard for ethnic minorities, it is not difficult to imagine how much more intense it may be in a closed community that all too easily picks on anyone who can be identified as different or vulnerable. The tragic reality of how far prisoner racism can go was seen in early 2000 when the young Asian, Zahid Mubarek, 19, serving a three-month sentence at Feltham for a minor offence, was found dead from head injuries. His death was caused by the prisoner with whom he shared a cell who made no secret of his extreme right-wing views.

Bobbie, 18, is Afro-Caribbean and when we met he had been at Moorland for three months and had encountered people with similar views to Mubarek's killer. His pent-up anger and feelings of alienation were palpable:

'Oh yes there's racism all right among the prisoners and some just don't want to know you. If you're black that's it, they think you shouldn't exist. And it gets nasty all right. There are guys here with real right-wing ideas. They'll get you if they can and beat you up just 'cos they don't like you. The inmates on the wing who hate black people draw swastikas and stick them under your door, or they talk about how "you people" have no sexual standards ... it goes on all right and everyone knows but I don't see much being done.'

Susie, 16, an Afro-Caribbean serving 18 months at Holloway for drug smuggling, considered:

'When I first came I was really scared because there weren't many other black girls and several of the whites came up to me and said things like "You black chicks think you're really hard. Well you'll see it's not like that here." And some of them did say horrible things to do with my colour. But you know as I settled down and stopped being so frightened I heard white girls saying really nasty things to each other, and very personal things. So I don't know if it's really all racism or just a way of picking on something to make a person feel bad.'

On the other hand white prisoners may have to be separated for their own protection. Frances Crook, director of the Howard League for Penal Reform, notes:

'White inmates who are overtly racist may be separated because of their attitudes. It happened to a boy from one of the areas of South Wales who had strong British National Party and Nazi sympathies. I was visiting and I was told one boy was being held in a segregation unit for his own protection – he had come in with Nazi slogans tattooed all up his arm, and other white supremacist stuff. This was a prison with a lot of black boys and he was segregated otherwise he would have been beaten up.'

Some officers I talked to believed segregation was most needed to keep different 'tribes' separated. One at Lancaster Farms raised his eyebrows as he explained: 'You can't put kids from Manchester and Liverpool in the same cell and don't mix lads who support different football teams. If you get Welsh kids there can be problems and North and South can be an explosive mix. Sometimes I wonder if we all belong to the same human race.'

To Imran, 19, Bangladeshi, who was in Lancaster Farms for drug dealing, it is not only white prisoners but also ethnic minorities who create the divisions:

'I've not experienced much racism here from the white prisoners but if there's a group of black people – Afro-Caribbeans and Asians – laughing and joking they expect me to join in. When I first arrived I got the impression off the black inmates that you all stick together, but I've been involved with a gang in the past and I don't want that over again, so I try just to keep myself to myself.'

Staff and race

In the first speech that Jack Straw gave as Home Secretary to the Prison Service Conference in 1998 he spoke powerfully of the need for the recruitment and retention of black and Asian staff. This speech seemed to herald a commitment by a government newly come to power to make sure things changed.

But by the year 2000 no more than a tiny proportion of those in officer and governor grades in all prisons were non-whites. Just over 2.5% of a total of 24,186 of these key members of staff, directly involved with and responsible for the welfare of ethnic minority inmates, were black, Asian or from other racial groups.[6] This is something young prisoners feel keenly. Black and Asian inmates in YOIs complain that there are so few officers of their colour and creed in the system.

Sabrina, 17, in Holloway on a charge of assault, puts it like this:

'If I got a problem as a black woman then I want to be able to talk to someone who understands where I am coming from. Don't matter whether it's to do with racism or not, I just feel I can trust a black woman more than a white woman and I don't think part of my punishment should be having to deal with people who don't understand what it means to be a black person.'

While Jiz, 18, a Muslim serving his sentence at Moorland, felt:

> 'There are special concerns around my religion, things I mind about that other prisoners don't, things that worry me and I feel if I say it to a white officer they won't understand but if there was a Muslim officer the fact he or she shared my way of seeing the world would mean I could talk out my problems.'

There is a widely held view that ethnic minorities face discrimination if they apply for jobs in the Prison Service and it is not surprising this may be a deterrent to joining up. But a trickier issue which needs addressing is how possible ethnic recruits feel about the way the prison system treats their own. Members of ethnic communities have spoken out about this, making it plain that they feel they would be supporting a system that discriminates and is inimical to justice for their young people. In a questionnaire designed to assess the problems black staff face one interviewee put it starkly: 'A job to be avoided – inhumane and authoritarian.'[7]

A white officer already working in the Service voiced the dilemma as he saw it: 'Some feel that if they come in here they'll be faced by this hostile group of black people saying, "Why are you here to lock me in? You're my brother or sister."' Another suggested black recruits might worry about being 'Uncle Toms'. They may, too, be secondary victims of racism, hearing officers refer to prisoners as 'coons', 'niggers' and so on.

Whatever the reasons, in 2000 the Prison Service admitted that throughout the entire Service there were just one Asian at a high governor grade and one Malaysian governor.

Clearly there are many issues to be addressed if the Prison Service is really serious about creating equality for ethnic minorities in prison and that means being proactive in considering how far racism may lead. Following the racist murder at Feltham in March 2000, a Prison Service report, quoted in *The Guardian* on 23 January 2001, concluded: 'That there is evidence that racism exists at Feltham, both overtly and by more subtle methods. Minority ethnic staff should not have to tolerate the level of harassment that exists in order to feel accepted as part of the team. Similarly, prisoners should be able to live free from racist abuse by staff.'

Paul McDowell, deputy governor of Feltham, talking in November 2001, says that tackling institutional racism has since been made an increased priority at Feltham: 'We have challenged racism here vigorously and really believe we have improved the situation a good deal, but I would be naive to say there is none. Changing a culture does take time.'

Bullying

Bullying is endemic in YOIs and although the weakest and most vulnerable are likely to suffer the worst, most young offenders (YOs) experience some form of bullying in prison.[8] Bullying is the way that some young people act out their feelings and attempt to gain status and a sense of power by controlling and intimidating other prisoners. For the victims it can seem that there is no escape. An objective assessment of how bad things are can be found in HM Chief Inspector's findings from Portland in 1999, where two out of five YOs had been threatened, one out of five with violence; 17% had been attacked and approximately 25% feared for their safety.[9] The number of YOs asking to be segregated for their own protection had almost doubled in the five months before Sir David's report was compiled.

Jim, 18, serving a sentence at Portland which he finished in 2000, describes how it was when a gang took against him in Portland:

'They would put dirt in my food, try to intimidate me into giving them my money and they hunted me down in the shower on several occasions to give me a beating. The worst was when they came in with batteries in socks – that's how a lot of beatings are given – and thrashed me. They broke several ribs and I was in agony but I didn't say anything because I knew that would make it worse. Also in Portland the officers didn't care. They quite liked prisoners fighting because the pecking order got sorted out and things were less trouble for them.'

Bullying takes different forms. Janine Morris, former deputy governor at Feltham, described shouting out of windows as one of the most invidious forms of bullying to take place because it is very personally threatening. Deeply hurtful things are said to vulnerable prisoners, as Morris explains:

'They shout constantly at each other for hour after hour and it gets very unpleasant. Then prisoners simmer all night and get into fights the next day. The worst is when someone insults a prisoner's mother, even though she may not even be around – they're very protective of their mothers. I remember one little chap who was beside himself because of some abuse that had been shouted. He said: "I wasn't going to put up with that stuff about my mother 'cos my mother died before I was conceived." I had to laugh at that, although not in front of him of course, but I also had to try to help him get moved from the boys who were making him wretched.'

Many prisoners describe other kinds of cruelty and persecution that are considered routine forms of bullying. Suliman at Lancaster Farms described how if a prisoner 'grassed up' another inmate, if they were a rapist or child abuser, or if they refused to do what a stronger prisoner, or one of a gang, demanded, they would get 'the treatment':

'You get glass ground into your food; inmates get slashed with the razor blades given out in the mornings and if they're not collected people keep them. The simplest weapon and it does the most damage is a cup of boiling water with sugar in it thrown into someone's face. The threat of that alone usually works. If someone is known to be scared or weak there's guys will take tobacco off them. I've seen people broken by all this. It surprises me there aren't more suicides although of course you don't hear about all the attempts.'

At Styal the prison psychologist Mike Jennings saw the power struggles between the girls and young women who so often feel powerless in their own lives:

'In the more chaotic houses there are people who you can see are frightened but they won't say why. The trouble with bullying is that someone doesn't have to be assaulted. If they are living with constant nastiness, threats, having their confidence eroded but no offence has been committed it's difficult for staff to step in and stop it. Whether it is this more subtle form or the classic vicious bullying, what you see is that the person who has been powerless and humiliated will take out their suffering by bullying someone weaker when they get the chance.'

So, in these institutions bullying reinforces a view of the world as a place where the toughest and hardest win and are respected. It is not difficult to see, then, how a prison subculture develops and if bullying goes unchecked it can create no-go areas in the prison. In these circumstances it is all too easy for staff to lose control. But conversely in prisons where staff use intimidation and bullying themselves to manage and control young people, bullying is more likely to occur.[10] However, bullying in prison is particularly difficult for staff to deal with, not least because prisoners are so loath to tell. Of all the taboos among young inmates, being a 'grass' is top of the list and the penalty for 'grassing' can be very high. It is seen as one of the reasons YOs become suicidal.

All prisons are required to have an anti-bullying strategy and a central principle is that bullying is tackled definitively and immediately it is discovered. Bullies should be put on offending behaviour programmes designed to get them to confront what they are doing and how it affects their victims. It is important that staff show they are absolutely supportive of the victim, at the same time looking to see what it is in his or her behaviour that may elicit bullying and whether skills training is needed.[11]

At Moorland a member of staff described the dedicated anti-bullying measures that David Waplington brought in when he was governor:

'He created a full-time anti-bullying officer whose job was to look out for signs of bullying. You see it in body language, when someone seems unhappy, and younger inmates are sometimes used by older ones to do the bullying for them. You have to understand how things work. If the officer thought there was a case of bullying he would ring me, then I'd go down and chat to people on the wing but always discreetly. We encourage everyone to report bullies and they can do it anonymously.'

Soon after the measures were introduced incidence of bullying dropped to 25 a month from more than twice that when Waplington arrived (he has since been moved on).

A senior officer at Styal remembers:

'One of our new very young inmates had a lot of attitude ... loud, swaggering and boastful. It was about the worst way possible to behave but any fool could see she was terrified underneath. Of course the other inmates don't understand that and there was a group of girls who really took against her. It wasn't like with boys, they didn't duff her over or pour aggression over her – things that are relatively easy to spot. No, whenever there was association or a time when staff weren't too much around them, these girls would call her hideous names, they told her that her boyfriend was with someone else, they told her she smelt, that nobody would ever like her ... an absolute onslaught of stuff and not surprisingly she cracked. She cut herself and it was only when I sat down and talked with her that it came out. In fact once I knew I could confront the girls doing it and I actually got them to see how it would feel if they were treated that way and to understand that the new girl was very frightened and unhappy. Then they calmed down.'

Lancaster Farms is a YOI where they put the tackling of bullying at the top of their priorities under governor David Thomas. Here learning about the anti-bullying strategy forms part of the induction package and inmates are asked to sign an agreement not to take part in bullying. If they refuse they are not eligible for privileges. There is an anti-bullying committee and inmates are encouraged to raise points which they see as helping to keep a positive regime. Victims are encouraged to come forward in the knowledge that their complaint will remain confidential, and bullies are segregated, as they are in many YOIs. Lancaster Farms is seen as having been strikingly successful in reducing bullying, a view endorsed by a number of prisoners who spoke to me.

Prisoners are quick to tell tales, as they have here, of officers ignoring bullying or sneering if instances of bullying are reported to them, but others, notably at Lancaster Farms and Huntercombe, talked of staff members who looked out for bullying and tried to deal with it. Darren, 18, who is small and has learning difficulties, told how, at Lancaster Farms:

> 'Someone must have spotted that I was having a bad time with this one boy who would take my canteen, threaten me when he saw me and he punched me a couple of times. I didn't say nothing – well you wouldn't – but he was taken off the wing and things got a lot better for me.'

Bullying is not of course confined to prisoner on prisoner. Cases the Howard League took up where inmates in one YOI claimed assault by officers are extreme examples of perceived bullying by staff and plenty of young prisoners described to me being given a cuff around the ear, a shove, designed to 'keep us in line' or because 'they just don't like me' as two inmates put it. But it is often subtler than this – psychological rather than physical assault – and often this can prove at least as damaging.

Joe, 18, at Moorland for manslaughter, described how:

> 'There was one officer who really took against me. A right bastard he was, but he didn't risk being caught doing anything that would get him into trouble. Instead he seemed to take every chance he could to make me look a fool in front of the other guys. He'd tell me someone had been into my cell and how it stank because I'd just used the loo … he'd suggest I was a loser with women … he would laugh at the way I do my hair … little things but they add up and it made me feel really screwed up and he'd say things like "can't imagine you making it outside, sonny".'

Prisoners should clearly be prevented from trying to gain power over others by bullying, but to tackle this problem effectively governors must be able to deal with officers who believe they have carte blanche to treat young inmates as they wish. Governors I spoke to all reported that they could get rid of members of staff they were unhappy with only if they were able to prove actual maltreatment of prisoners.

It is not possible to have a truly rehabilitative ethos in a prison where any kind of sustained bullying is allowed to exist. The effect of bullying is insidious, undermining and a form of punishment that in no way accords with what a sentence is intended to be. If it is not dealt with the chances are that YOs who have got away with bullying will continue to bully, or worse, outside.

Mental health

Sam, 20, sits in his cell, head bowed, talking in a flat, sad voice about the night he lost control in a psychotic breakdown and killed his mother:

'It comes flooding back over and over and the bad memories, sudden flashes, are very clear. I want to remember the good things like my Mum's face but I can't, and I can't make sense of any of it. All this drains me and I feel very, very miserable inside. Oh yes I've attempted suicide and I still think of it often, because I'm so mad and muddled inside.'

In prison they have told Sam he should talk to the psychologist and not block things out but he didn't feel he wanted to go over it all with her. He was then given a bad psychological report: 'That made me angry and I told the psychologist what she said was wrong and it makes me feel more alone and that I don't know how I'll cope with it all in my head.'

This young man is not alone in struggling with mental health problems. Of the children and young people placed in custody a much higher ratio suffer from mental health illness than in the general population. Even so the courts send them into a prison environment although just about every governor I spoke to made the point that prisons are not equipped to deal with the needs of particularly disturbed and vulnerable YOs.

In a 1997 survey more than 90% of imprisoned YOs in England and Wales showed evidence of suffering from at least one of a range of disturbances.[12] Often mental illness, or mental instability as a result of substance addiction, or difficulties in functioning such as hyperactivity and autism, are found in young people who end up in prison. They have high levels of anxiety, depression, fatigue, concentration problems and suicidal feelings. A sense of overwhelming hopelessness is common.

Carrie, 16, in Styal for stealing, was put into care at the age of 12, when her mother left her father and set up home with another man who made it plain he did not want the daughter as well. Several foster placements broke down when she came home drunk, was abusive, and would not change her behaviour:

'I started drinking when I went into care. I bunked off school and nicked drink from off-licences. The drink was good because it stopped me feeling so upset about my Mum. Social workers tried a bit to help me, and a doctor gave me tranquillisers because I wasn't sleeping and I was getting very nervous and twitchy. But once I turned 16 I went and slept on the streets and that's not good for your head. It's probably as well they've locked me up – might be dead otherwise – but I don't know how I can ever sort myself out.'

At Holloway, which receives the majority of serious psychiatric cases, numbers of girls and young women coming into the prison rose steadily after the introduction of the Detention and Training Order (DTO) (see page 23). The governor, David Lancaster, talked despairingly of how the Crime and Disorder Act 1998 was supposed to mean that fewer juveniles would end up in custody, not more. The prison had not received extra money even though he was well aware he had prisoners who should be given appropriate help: 'Prison is not the right place for people with severe and complicated problems. Even here with a psychiatric wing and a strong medical team we do not have the specialised resources to look after these very sad young women.' Early in 2001 two young women took their lives in Holloway. In each case Lancaster believes that an environment equipped to deal with their mental health problems might well have prevented their deaths.

Chris Tchaikovsky, director of Women in Prison, has seen how tough it can be for the mentally disturbed young when they are locked up with better-functioning peers:

'They have the worst time inside because they are at the bottom of the bucket, boys and girls. Their vulnerability and desire to make friends is spotted instantly and exploited. They get everything taken off them and friendships are offered with all kinds of appalling conditions attached. Mental illness is so often a product of people being hurt, neglected and abused in life, then prison compounds all that. Can those in charge of penal policy really believe they are going to turn out kids better able to function in the world, this way?'

Marcia Williams, appointed as health adviser at the then newly opened Holloway YO unit in 1998 (but closed in mid-2001, see page 108) came into contact with 40 young women aged 15–21 serving sentences ranging from a month to life. Emotional fragility was what she found, almost always stemming from events that had upset their emotional and mental equilibrium. Summing up her findings and the work done after one year Williams talked to me of how deeply distressing it was to hear the women's stories:[13]

'During the first six months I felt overwhelmed by the volume of emotional trauma expressed by these women. I heard many stories of homeless young women having worked on the streets from the age of 13, young women abused sexually by peers, partners, strangers and family members and stories from girls with a history of abuse while in local authority care. All this highlights in my mind how society has failed these young women in achieving even their basic needs such as shelter, warmth and loving relationships and it is hardly surprising they fail to cope in the most fundamental way.'

Every governor I spoke to for this book talked similarly about how they inherit a proportion of inmates with a lifetime of the most disturbing experiences and disturbed responses which makes their job almost impossibly difficult at times. And although offending is not a mental health problem in itself, young people may well offend because they are struggling with such problems and failing to cope with life as the more stable do.[14] Nor is it surprising that, once these young people have offended and been put into prison, they may be pushed further into chaos if, for example, they are locked up for long hours in a cell with someone they cannot get along with or if they become a victim of bullying.

One of the difficulties even when help is available is the reluctance of young prisoners to talk about emotional and mental health difficulties given the considerable stigma attached to doing so.

The past life of Doug, 20, now out of prison, is a series of losses through death and divorce, culminating in his fiancée dying when he was 18. He had lived in a 'kind of twilight state thinking everyone I met was going to rob me or beat me up or in some way harm me'. He began taking drugs, graduated to heroin and, unable to afford his fix, broke into a chemist's and threatened the owner with a syringe full of blood, claiming it was infected.

> 'I don't really remember much about that night. I hadn't slept for a time, I was very paranoid by that time, watching my back whenever I went out and angry with everyone. I didn't eat and I didn't speak to anybody. When I got to prison and off the heroin I wanted to talk about the feelings that were inside me because it still worried me, but I knew if I said anything it would get around the wing somehow and then they'd see me as weird, a screwball, so I just shut up.'

Mental health training is a component of the general staff training, but Marcia Williams was a particularly innovative appointment at Holloway. Her role involved identifying the physical and mental health needs of inmates and then attempting to look at how they could be met both by her and by other available staff. One of the most pressing kinds of help needed, she felt, was enabling women to talk about their deep-seated problems. Here she realised that they did not want to do it face to face. Instead they chose to be separated by a door and to be counselled via the hatch opening. The specialised understanding she brought with her of how unstable youngsters may want to 'protect' their distress enabled her to see that the same young woman who was desperate with her problems during counselling could appear carefree, happy and even bolshie and troublesome later during normal activities. But Williams understood this did not mean she was 'cured'. Often each private session would bring up new pain and upset.

Other prisons buy in psychiatric help and use volunteer counselling. But it is too little and too ad hoc in the face of so much mental distress festering in our youth prisons. It is with this in mind that David Waplington, who recalls 'a great deal of depression, anxiety and minor mental health illness in every YOI' he has seen wants to make use of his new role, as head of the Juvenile Offender Group at Prison Service Headquarters, to get 'a whole range of well-being support services' put in place.

Suicide and self-harm

Sixteen 15–21 year olds killed themselves in prison during 2000 in England and Wales and in the decade between 1990 and 2000 the total number was more than 60, according to the campaigning organisation Inquest. It would be shocking enough if these children and young people took their lives on the outside, but it is yet more so when the state takes on the role of carer and then provides such inadequate care that young inmates choose to commit suicide.

Young men are more likely to kill themselves than young women, but in conversation they are a great deal less keen to talk about having suicidal thoughts. Several told me firmly that it doesn't look good, you might be called 'a Fraggle' if you admit to that kind of vulnerability (the name comes from the TV series *Fraggle Rock*, which featured the Muppets, seen in inmate culture as derisory characters). But Sam, at Moorland, told me he had attempted suicide several times after being convicted of the murder of his mother, before he was sentenced, and he had frequently thought about it since being found guilty of murder: 'It wouldn't be easy here but it's possible, people find ways and there are days I feel so bad I just think I'll bang my head on the wall till it splits. I've been on suicide watch a couple of times but as you can see I haven't done it yet.'

Officers know well that a letter with bad news, the death of someone loved whom a prisoner has not said goodbye to, knowledge that a partner is leaving them are all things that can make a prisoner feel suicidal.

Mimi, 16, was serving a three-year sentence for grievous bodily harm, at Styal. She is a small, wiry girl with a fierce expression, who was put into care aged six – her parents never visited even though they lived close by. She gives a small smile as she says: 'I went through foster homes like a dose o' salts, I did.' The only friends she had were a group of girls with similar histories:

'Nobody cared I was out of school so I never learnt anything. Then I ended up in here and I had to come down from the drinks and drugs I'd been using and suddenly it hit me. I'm shit. Just shit. No good to anyone. I didn't want to mix with anyone, I just wanted to get my head down and do my time. Then one afternoon I got a phone call from someone back home saying me best mate had been killed in a car crash. You know what, she was the only person in the world who gave a damn about me, thought I was okay. Well I just went AWOL, didn't see any point in anything and all I wanted was to die and if I could have found a way then I'd have done it.'

Suicide, like self-harm, is an act of desperation. The fact that almost half of all deaths in prison occur within one month of reception into custody is a measure of just how shocking and frightening prison can be to a vulnerable young person when they first arrive and panic at the idea of having to cope.[15] Inmates who take their lives are said to fall into two categories. The long-term prisoners, often lifers, who tend to be in the upper age-group, kill themselves out of a sense of guilt for the offence and a feeling that they have no future. The poor copers, who are generally younger and in for less serious offences, and the mentally ill tend to commit suicide out of feelings of despair, fear, helplessness and isolation. They may suffer far more than the older prisoners from being separated from family and friends, from bullying and the shock of being locked up.[16]

A member of staff who believes a YO may take their life can register them as 'at risk' and the inmate may be put on a 15-minute watch. It is, however, a much-voiced view that this is not enough and that truly vulnerable youngsters need to be on full-time watch and ideally with someone who will attempt to help them with whatever problem or feelings have pushed them to this dangerous state. What may happen is that they are put on a 24-hour watch by someone outside the cell, but this offers little comfort and none of the informal counselling which would be possible with somebody keeping the prisoner company. It is also a very costly system as usually the watcher has to be bought in from an outside agency and, with the budget constraints every prison governor spoke about, this is likely to be done only when the risk of suicide seems considerable.

Abbie, 16, in Holloway for a drug offence, was put on suicide watch:

'I was feeling really bad thinking about my Mum. She won't come and see me here. She said to me when I was sentenced, "I told you before you got into all that crap that you'd be on your own, I'm not coming to see you." I can understand it would hurt her to see me here. I shouldn't have let it get to me that bad, but sometimes it just does 'cos I really want to talk to my Mum. If I could have killed myself then I would have. But an officer had a chat and really listened to me while I was on watch and that kind of got me out of it.'

When a young person who has been incarcerated does succeed in killing themself there is shock and outrage. The suicide of Phillip Griffin, 17, who was serving a 10-month sentence for burglary and robbery in Wetherby YOI and who killed himself a few weeks into his sentence, was reported as a scandal by the media. The Children's Society backed Sir David Ramsbotham's call on the government to stop imprisoning under-18 year olds. Yet although the courts have access to all the evidence on the dangers of locking up vulnerable children they still choose to do so. The case of Phillip Griffin illustrates this as well as any. He was homeless and his family 'washed their hands of him' when they heard that he had burgled a house. Despite evidence given and anxieties expressed by Griffin's lawyer that Griffin 'didn't seem stable' he was sent to prison and within a few weeks he was dead.

The reasons young people in prison take their lives are complex, acknowledges Deb Coles, director of Inquest, which investigates cases of suicide, but she also thinks it is 'no coincidence' that they are concentrated in those YOIs that have the most impoverished, repressive regimes and conditions:

> 'The reality of imprisonment for many of the young people who have killed themselves is boredom, isolation, drug or alcohol withdrawal and a prison environment that exacerbates suicidal feelings. Inactive, impersonal regimes create a hostile and punitive environment. Too often there is a failure to respond to bullying.'

Furthermore, she asserts, suicide prevention strategies, suicide screening checks and proper attention to psychiatric and medical health needs are regularly disregarded: 'What is so depressing is the inaction of successive governments to the crisis of an ever-escalating death rate and the high incidence of self-harm.'

Self-harm

Lisa, 16, began cutting herself 'to get rid of the hurt inside me' when she was 10, but she had stopped for three years before she was sent to Holloway for burglary: 'Being in my cell, shut up, all the bad feelings came back. So I started again ...'

Self-harm most often means cutting, where inmates find a sharp object – for boys it is often a razor they have managed to hide away – and slash at wrists and arms although it can be all over the body, and either surface cuts or deep gashes. But it may also be head-banging, pulling out hair, gouging the flesh and swallowing objects such as batteries.

In 1997 there were 7,023 recorded incidences of self-harm in prisons in England and Wales involving 5,552 prisoners, including juveniles and older YOs.[17] Girls and young women harm themselves more than males, according to the Home Office. It happens in every YOI and, not surprisingly in a prison with the problems and stresses of Feltham, Janine Morris, when deputy governor, experienced this phenomenon all too often:

> 'We have young people in the hospital unit who constantly cut themselves all over – one lad has managed to cut right down through the tendon and as it heals he bites through it again. They need a great deal of help, more than we are equipped to give, but the courts keep on sending them to us.'

When prison officers describe self-harming behaviour as 'attention-seeking' they may mean they see the prisoner as manipulative and wanting special treatment. I found others who were sympathetic. There are staff who dislike the way attention-seeking is talked of as an impermissible thing to do. Lorraine Holt at Styal was one:

'A lot of our girls have no idea how to express their unhappiness in an appropriate way. They've never learned that they can take their problems to an adult, have them listened to and taken seriously. A lot have learned instead that it's negative behaviour that gets attention. If they were naughty as kids or got into trouble there would be anger, physical violence, all very negative attention, but they say it's better than when nobody takes any notice of you. So I don't see attention-seeking as them calculating that they'll get what they want. Rather I see it as the most desperate way of saying please notice my pain.'

David Lancaster, governor of Holloway, knows it is impossible to stop self-mutilation but compassion, he says, is essential:

'We have to ask ourselves what is motivating these young people. Many have suffered abuse and all kinds of neglect that have left them feeling very bad about themselves, guilty for what they have allowed to happen to them in their lives – even though those of us outside can, of course, see that it wasn't their fault. The feelings overwhelm them and many talk of getting some kind of release when they cut themselves. That is not ideal and I would like to think we can help them to find better ways to get out their bad feelings, but whatever else we need to understand and treat them decently and that is what I expect of my staff.'

When children and young people are sent to prison, supposedly as a last resort, the intention is that they receive constructive punishment with rehabilitation as its goal.[18] Given that the government is bound by child welfare and human rights legislation, the fact that so many YOs should feel driven to these desperate measures is a reason to question whether they should be sent to prison.[19] Paul McDowell, deputy governor at Feltham, puts it this way:

'Nobody could accuse us of treating them as children. You can pretty it up in whatever way you like but we are putting these vulnerable kids into a place with a big fence and barbed wire on top. There are people in charge who have been working in the service for years and may not have ideas that tally with popular notions of child development and they are expected to cope in a pretty tough macho world of their peers. If it was your kids, would you think it was treating them as children should be treated?'

NOTES

1. 'The wholly unacceptable treatment and conditions for young offenders, including children, which are far removed from the published intentions of the Government, the Prison Service and the Youth Justice Board. Unacceptably it discloses that many of the improvements and advances, made elsewhere in recent years, appear to have passed or been allowed to pass the establishment by.' *HM Young Offender Institution Portland: Report of a full announced inspection by HM Chief Inspector of Prisons*. London, Home Office, 1999.

2. *Prison Statistics, England and Wales*. London, Home Office, 2000; *Estimates of the Population by Ethnic Group and Area of Residence, England and Wales*. London, Office for National Statistics, 2000.

3. *Howard League Factsheet 9: Ethnic minorities and the criminal justice system* (based on 1995 government figures). London, Howard League for Penal Reform, 2000.

4. Gordon Berkely: *Ethnic Differences in Decisions on Young Defendants dealt with by the Prosecution Service*. London, Home Office, 1997.

5. *Ibid*.

6. 97.4% white, 1.5% black, 0.7% Asian and 0.4% other; Robin Alfred, *Black Workers in the Prison Service*. London, Prison Reform Trust, 1992.

7. *Ibid*.

8. *Banged Up, Beaten Up, Cutting Up: The report of the Howard League Commission of Inquiry into violence in penal institutions for teenagers under 18*. London, Howard League for Penal Reform, 1995.

9. See note 1.

10. Kevin Browne and Louise Falshaw, 'Factors Relating to Bullying in Secure Accommodation', *Child Abuse Review*, Vol. 5, Issue 2, May 1996.

11. *Ibid*.

12. Nicola Singleton *et al.*, *Psychiatric Morbidity among Prisoners in England and Wales*. London, Office for National Statistics, 1997.

13. Marcia Williams, *A Year in Holloway Young Offenders Unit: Health visiting in a custodial environment*. London, HM Prison Service, 1999.

14. Michael Rutter, Henri Giller and Ann Hagell, *Antisocial Behaviour by Young People: The main messages from a major new review of research*. London, Policy Research Bureau, 1998.

15. Graham Towl, ed., 'Suicide and Self-Injury in Prisons: Research directions in the 1990s', *Issues in Criminological and Legal Psychology*, No. 28, 1996, reviewed in *Prison Service Journal*, No. 116, March 1998.

16. Alison Liebling, *Suicides in Prisons*. London, Routledge, 1992.

17. See note 12.

18. Crime and Disorder Act 1998.

19. The UN Convention on the Rights of the Child 1991; the Human Rights Act 1998; and the Children's Act 1989.

'I have been given an opportunity to create the regime I think can be constructive – I call it a Whole Prison Approach and it is about treating people with respect, openness, fairness. getting them to take responsibility for their actions, encouraging them, praising them. And this approach should be like a stick of rock so that wherever you break it you will still read the same message.'

Paul Mainwaring, governor of Huntercombe YOI

6 Prisons fit for our children

As with the lives of so many young offenders Robbie's childhood taught him that 'in life there are only a few people who are true'. His mother, an alcoholic, was 16 when he was born. There were four sisters, and a brother who died; then his parents split up. All the children were put into care. He saw neither parent again (his mother is now dead) until he made contact with his father, while last in prison, but their contact is limited. Now that he is out, Robbie talks with cool articulacy of how he saw himself as an outsider, of no value to anyone. So it startled him to find a prison that seemed to be 'on my side rather than treating me like the scum of the earth' when, aged 18, he was sent to serve a one-year sentence at Huntercombe:

'Huntercombe felt different to other prisons and people were nicer to you, but it didn't add up. I was still trouble but I was moved onto a wing with this officer, an older woman who liked me, and that was lucky – I can't speak highly enough of her. When she came on duty she would come and see how I was and she got me a little paid job in the library. She did lots of little things that made a real difference for me and it made me feel she cared about me, that I mattered. I was fascinated with computers and she and Steive Butler got me on to a computer course. It was so beautiful I was able to do all these things with computers. I told everyone at college that I was from prison and if they showed some trust that was great. I did brilliantly on the course which made me proud for that officer. Then Steive Butler got me the chance to desktop-publish the prison magazine and take photos for it. I'm dead proud of what I've managed to do with that and it gives me a sense I can do something other than crime. I want to work with computers and go on making friends like I did at college with people who aren't into crime. But that change wouldn't have happened without my being sent to Huntercombe.'

James, 18, had a very different experience when he served time at a young offender institution (YOI) that he doesn't want to name in case he is sent there again: 'The whole attitude was that we were all the same and not worth bothering with. That went right through education, PE, the way most of the screws talked to you. I just felt they wanted us to get through time and not be trouble. Rehabilitation? Don't make me laugh.'

These two young men illustrate how different the experience of prison may be, depending on the ethos of the place and the way its inmates are regarded. It also suggests that a constructive, humane regime will stand a better chance of sending offenders out with the will not to reoffend.

From self-esteem to skills

Setting aside for the moment the central argument about whether most of the children and young people who end up in prison really should be there, the purpose of this chapter is to consider what it may be possible to achieve with young inmates. I have spent time looking at YOIs which came up frequently as examples of good or bad practice, but the focus here is on what is constructive, because it seems to me most important that we understand what, at best, can be done for children and young people in prison.

The idea that time and money should be spent on providing better conditions for young offenders (YOs) tends to be seen as something taxpayers will balk at if they understand what it costs. But David Thomas, governor at the award-winning Lancaster Farms, which was commended by Sir David Ramsbotham, HM Chief Inspector of Prisons at the time, for its 'caring and supportive culture for inmates' and by the Prison Reform Trust for its good practice, explains:

'We have to help the public understand that humane and decent prisons where the inmates feel you want to help them live better lives, and that they matter as people, actually protect the next victim. Risk assessment and management of that risk is always our bottom line, but the young person who walks out the prison gates having learnt to control their anger, their impulsiveness, to like themselves a bit better than they did when they came in and feeling staff valued them enough to help them go out with a few more skills than they brought in, is less likely to go off and harm someone. Of course even the best of regimes don't prevent enough YOs from returning to crime but I do believe they send people out less likely to commit violent crimes than if they've been through a harsh and punitive regime where they return to the community with low self-esteem and a lot of pent-up anger.'

The ethos

The governors I spoke with expressed a similar belief, that a good prison ethos has at its heart the welfare and development of its young charges. It is important that the staff are enthusiastic and supportive of the philosophy of the way the prison is run.

Anyone who has read the grim news that regularly surfaces about conditions and treatment of young people in some YOIs will have no illusions about how often this goal has not been met. When David Waplington took over as governor at Moorland, it was a prison with a reputation for violence among inmates, and had in Waplington's words an 'unproductive regime' where 'discipline was always emphasised'. What happened under his leadership is an illustration of how profoundly prison ethos may be affected by the way a governor runs things. Waplington describes Moorland when he first arrived in the mid-1990s:

> 'You couldn't walk around the place without having things screamed at you. I was regularly called a four-eyed c***! But that was nothing compared to what the female staff got. What I inherited there in the way of an ethos and a regime was the worst I had seen in the service. The whole place was looking backwards and I knew I had to change everything from top to bottom if we were going to do the thing I believe is essential and treat prisoners with respect from the minute they come through the door. As well as having faith in their ability to change and improve.'

Under Waplington's governorship – he was promoted and left at the end of 1999 – there was a reduction in violent incidents and assaults at Moorland, which has been maintained subsequently.[1] Jacquie Pooley, who ran a YMCA unit for YOs there at the time, offering a place to go for advice, guidance and relaxation – for which Waplington had raised funding – spoke of how things had changed in her view:

> 'There was a big difference when David took over – it was a quite dramatic improvement in behaviour and morale among the lads as they realised they were being thought about and were important as people. The enhanced regime was introduced, a new wing built and inmates had more time out of cells. Before it was a very strict regime where, if you stepped out of line, that was it. David insisted on rules being obeyed but his way is to try to help the lads see that learning to behave and fit into a regime is a skill that will benefit them outside.'

The bottom line for David Thomas, governor at Lancaster Farms, is that no matter what an offender has done, they are punished by the courts with loss of liberty, and the prison's job is to do the best it can in the way of rehabilitation, not add further punishment to the sentence. His ideas are not universally shared:

> 'Some of my staff believe that if we were harder on inmates it would be more of a deterrent. The trouble is, that legitimises so many things that are unacceptable in a civilised society. There is also now much evidence to show that you don't modify behaviour through punishment but through enabling people to take responsibility for themselves.'

Governors

A positive ethos depends to a very large extent, then, on the attitude of governors and their staff. The way they think and behave can be instrumental in teaching young inmates who have often trusted few if any adults, that they can safely do so – although it should be said that all the inmates I spoke to distinguished between those members of staff they had found caring and trustworthy and those who in their view had no interest, or basically disliked them all. So inmates in the best of the prisons visited referred to governors in such terms as 'really safe' and in Holloway one girl said of David Lancaster: 'He's very straight, but not a bad guy. Has a minute for you.'

Steive Butler, arts coordinator at Huntercombe, which used to have all YOs but now has only juveniles, described the approach of governor Paul Mainwaring who had worked as a psychiatric nurse earlier in his career:

> 'I see him running the prison almost like an extended family. The idea is to let the lads see that things here are what normal life should be and that means showing, and expecting to receive, respect, and taking on responsibilities. Paul is firm and of course there is punishment when essential, but his way is to treat the inmates a bit like valued sons. So when, for example, there's an important football match he will say, "Let's get the lads out to watch", and he'll organise tins of soft drinks.'

There have been a few exceptionally humane and imaginative governors running YOIs for some years. However, when the youth justice reforms were brought in, new breed reforming governors were put in place in a number of prisons earmarked to take juveniles, or encouraged to stay, to make sure that the welfare-based juvenile estate was properly delivered. But much good work is undermined when enlightened governors are moved on, often after a year or two, or three at most, when their measures, particularly radical ones, may be beginning to take effect. Of course the reverse may happen too and old-style governors be replaced by better people. The all too frequent moving-on of governors who have won the respect, cooperation and liking even of their young charges, has a very negative impact on staff and inmates.

Recognising this, Paul Mainwaring told the Prison Service when he took over at Huntercombe that he intended to stay for at least four years, and David Thomas was at Lancaster Farms for several years. But Mainwaring is aware that it is a lot to ask of people to sacrifice prestige and higher pay for the greater good of prisoners: 'It's time this way of doing things was re-thought at the top. Why can't they have a scheme where governors like myself can be promoted by perhaps having something added to our title and our pay upgraded while remaining in the same job? Everyone would win that way.'

The regime

The regime is the pattern and routine of life which shapes and, ideally, develops the lives of YOs. The quality and quantity of what is currently offered varies greatly. In the view of several governors I spoke to, a good regime will offer a dynamic and full programme of activities which are demanding and stimulating and where there is potential for enjoyment as well as concern for child welfare. Larry Wright, manager of the Hammersmith and Fulham Youth Offending Team (YOT), has been struck by the positive attitudes of many of the children his team deal with when they leave Huntercombe. He compares this with the inward-looking negativity of YOs leaving Feltham:

> 'There is such a marked difference between what the two places perceive as achievable. We do not at present advocate custody but I believe the time will come, if places like Huntercombe can continue to offer kids a humane regime and opportunities they can't or won't take up outside, that we might in essential cases advocate the use of such regimes.'

David Waplington describes his priorities when he took over as governor of the YOI at Moorland:

> 'To start with we needed activities because there were none. A good education department was critical, partly because many inmates come in handicapped by lack of education and if anything will help them get out of the crime loop it is that. But also education departments can be good places for building trusting relationships between prisoners and staff. I raised money to bring in a musician and get musical equipment. Music is one of the most effective ways of helping those who have been lost by formal education and is a very good way of reaching prisoners

with mental health problems. They find they can be good at something unthreatening. I watched the confidence of these inadequate young-sters soar in some cases.

'I also looked at things like PE and at how inmates communicated on association. Everything on offer had to feel as though it prioritised the lads' well-being and progress. If you shove people into cells, say "get on with it" and leave them to find their own way through the systems they will say, "they don't care about me in this place so I won't do what they suggest or want". That way you get into the cycle of anger, fear and depression.'

Barry Denton, deputy at Moorland before he moved to Feltham in spring 2001 to take charge of the older YOs there, described how he came to understand the importance of a positive regime:

'Doing this job has been a road to Damascus conversion for me. I started out believing that what you had to do was teach the youngsters who was boss and kick them into shape. But once I started hearing the lads' stories, seeing how lost and helpless so many seemed and how they needed decent parenting so badly, I changed my views com-pletely. The point of a regime, as I see it, is to set up the kind of struc-ture, requirements, discipline and motivation that good parents do for their kids. They need to see that they must stop their antisocial behav-iour because they will have better lives if they do. They need teaching how to live in a more social-minded way and they need to see that it is up to them to make the decision to do so.'

At Lancaster Farms David Thomas began as deputy governor, and during this time he and the governor spent six months looking at what was being done elsewhere with young inmates. Thomas explains:

'At Feltham they were killing themselves, in other places violence was prevalent and there were such abusive power structures – fear and loathing were endemic. Our view was that it shouldn't have to be like this for the public to be protected – besides, these grim, punitive regimes had high reoffending rates. I felt we should be creating a prison fit for our own children.'

The regime is structured around activities but human relations are absolutely key to the way it is delivered and how day-to-day life is experi-enced by prisoners. To Michael Selby, a former prison governor, certain active steps have to be taken in order to set up a positive regime:

'It is as well to start with a basic rule of managing a prison … staff should actually talk to prisoners and also, incidentally, to each other.

This does not happen in many prisons. It is just a matter of one human being talking to another as a matter of course, on trivial matters, as well as important. For some prisons this will require a culture shock, but until it is done, nothing else can happen. Conversation is the foundation of any regime.'

Purposeful activity

A typical day for young prisoners will depend on how the regime is set up, but juveniles on Detention and Training Orders (DTOs) are required by law to have 30 hours of 'purposeful activity' a week, with a maximum of 11 hours a day, which includes formal education, offending behaviour courses, sports and other organised activities. School-age children must have 15 hours' education a week, ideally at least two hours a week of PE, although this may not always happen, and one hour a day, at least, of recreation and association.

Prisons are not required to provide such a full-time regime for older YOs, although education either as private study or classes is supposed to be available to those beyond school age who want it, or they may choose to do prison work or work training instead. The government recorded that in the year 1999–2000 some YOIs offered just 15.2 hours a week of purposeful activity out of cell although the best offered more than 30 hours a week. At Feltham in 1999 the average time out of cell was just 3.29 hours per day for sentenced prisoners aged 18–21 years, but by the end of 2001 the situation had improved and purposeful activity for older YOs had been increased from 12 to 22 hours, for both remand and sentenced prisoners.[2]

It is not difficult to see how little education, exercise and activities prisoners in the YO estate may have and it is not surprising that there are complaints about too much time being spent 'banged up'. Humanitarian concerns aside, such purposeless incarceration is counter-productive. A shortage of resources for the older age-group often makes it hard for governors to provide the regimes they would like, and this may mean insufficient facilities to meet the needs of an often over-crowded unit, or too few staff being available to take the YOs to education, the PE block or recreational activities. Even association is sometimes missed. Sickness, too, depletes staff quotas – often already operating without any margins.[3]

David Lancaster, governor at Holloway, is aware of how destructive 'idle time' may be and in spite of the difficulties, he strives to give the 18–21 year olds there a full regime:

'They get up at 7.00 am and they are out of their cells all morning for education and exercise, then back in their cells after lunch from 2.30 pm until 4.30 pm. Out again until about 8.00 pm. So during the weekdays they are out of cell a lot but at weekends there is no association and they are locked up from 5.30 pm until the next morning.'

A regime that has won considerable praise, including from Sir David Ramsbotham, is the pioneering High Intensity Training (HIT) programme at Thorn Cross in Cheshire, which has received considerable funding and appears to be having some success in reducing offending. It relies on a very full and active regime – the day beginning at 6.00 am and ending at 10.00 pm. The programme includes the same mix of education, activities, PE and offending behaviour work as other YOIs but evening classes are also built in. Although the day is rigorous and disciplined a therapeutic approach is integral and staff are given special psychological training before joining the HIT unit.

Planning time

The way a day is structured for a young prisoner depends to some extent on his or her sentence plan. This, as the name suggests, is a plan of action which should be drawn up by a group of people, or by a single officer, concerned with the prisoner's time in prison and after they are released – although in practice this is not always done for older YOs. For a juvenile on a DTO the sentence plan should have been made out by the YOT before they reach prison (and the risk of self-harm should have been assessed at the youth court as well as on arrival at prison). Within five days of arrival the first planning meeting should be held with the juvenile present. The aim of the planning procedure is to help the young prisoner to take a part in making decisions about what they will do with their time inside. The importance of finding something that they believe will be constructive is stressed, and they should also be involved in talking through which offending behaviour courses might be beneficial. At best a well-planned sentence with purposeful activities can give young inmates opportunities they did not have outside. Robbie recalls a 'couple of friends', also sentenced to time in Huntercombe, who illustrate this point:

> 'When they came in they were, quite honestly, thugs. They had been working very casually as bricklayers and although they started out kicking off something bad, once they had settled down and realised this isn't a bad place they built a fountain out the front of the prison. They also started studying and both went to college. One became a teacher and the other got an NVQ level three. They're both out now, working, earning good money and they're not angry all the time.'

But of course these transformations do not happen to everyone. Jeb, 17, at Lancaster Farms, seemed determined that prison would not offer him anything:

> 'I've gone to lessons 'cos I had to. I've taken part in activities, I've got along with other prisoners on association – I've kept my head down and

I'm regarded as a good prisoner but I've done nothing – *nothing* of value here and I won't have anything to take out that can offer me an alternative to living the way I have for years. And no, they haven't got to my heart. I've never thought about victims and I'm not likely to start now.'

Staff training

Persuading young people to change and reshape their behaviour depends a great deal on how staff deal with them. But for years the prison system required prison officers who might have worked with adults throughout their career to change over to working with young inmates without any additional training in child welfare or adolescent development.

As any parent of teenagers will know, children and young people see the world very differently from their elders, and their value systems and behaviour may well be very different too. So it is not surprising that working with them – particularly if they are angry and emotionally upset on top of the normal adolescent feelings – can be demanding and difficult.

It was with this in mind that the Trust for the Study of Adolescence (TSA) designed *The Nature of Adolescence*, a training pack for prison staff working with male juveniles. It was then adapted for girls and is now in the process of being revised for use with older YOs. By 1999, 3,500 officers and other prison staff had completed the 11-hour course. It is broken down into modules and is intended to help staff understand normal adolescent development and behaviour and differentiate between this and criminal behaviour. Juliet Lyon, who helped design the course while she was at TSA, says: 'We wanted to make prison staff aware of how far the inmates' behaviour is classic adolescent acting-out. And we wanted them to think back to their own experience of adolescence, to occasions when they had flouted authority and broken the law.'

Some staff objected when asked to do the training and a few told me they thought it a waste of time, but most, according to TSA evaluators, have been enthusiastic. David Thomas explains how it worked at Lancaster Farms where they pioneered the training:

'We start by asking staff to apply to work with young prisoners because it is something you have to want to do. Then everyone – absolutely everyone – who has contact with YOs, right to the tea-ladies, is put through the training package. It means there are no boundaries between different specialities or workers when it comes to understanding our inmates and it is a way we can all share information.'

A number of staff told me the training had helped them in their work. One, with 'many years' service under my belt', expressed a familiar thought – he had expected YOs to be easier than adult prisoners:

'How wrong can you be! Young offenders are demanding and their irrational adolescent behaviour is often irritating, time-consuming and frequently challenging in a way you don't want to have to deal with. My view is that those who don't want to work with YOs shouldn't be made to do so. But I'm happy to say that now I feel I've got to grips with the kids I really enjoy the opportunities for helping them change themselves and see they've a better life ahead. And they make me laugh!'

At Holloway a young officer then working with juveniles raised her well-groomed eyebrows high:

'The decibel count can go through the roof on the unit. When the girls are acting out or excited about something you'd think there was a wild tribe here. But the other side is they go very low and withdrawn when things are bad for them. I'm not very old myself and the training helped me to realise how lucky I was going through adolescence with just normal ups and downs and problems. At the same time it's given me the insight to be able to take a grown-up approach and be firm when necessary.'

Education

Suliman, 17 when sentenced, is not a sentimental young man. But he looks back to his secondary school days spent constantly bunking off, shoplifting, committing the occasional street robbery, driving away cars and taking pride in belonging to a gang known as 'bad boys', and he still cannot quite believe the way things have gone:

'Going to prison was the worst day of my life. There was my Mum in court crying her heart out. I couldn't comfort her and I was so frightened myself. But now I can honestly say, even taking account of the bullying and the bad things that went on, prison is the best thing that could have happened to me. I really don't think anything else would have stopped me because I was not thinking about any future.'

At Lancaster Farms Suliman, who spent the first months being so disruptive in class that he was told not to come to education, was given a second chance when he went back saying he wanted to study after receiving a letter from his mother asking why he didn't 'do something with my time inside'. Within two years he had made up for missed secondary years and taken six GCSEs, two A levels and been offered a place at university. 'I'd never have done it without the brilliant teachers at the Farms. They worked so hard with me so that my confidence grew. Now I have got a future and dreams like other people. I can imagine having a home, a wife, kids.'

Education is potentially one of the most important and empowering things prison can offer a young person because it gives them a chance, if they want to take it, of altering their destiny. But that possibility depends on good teaching and adequate resources being available for education. It also matters a great deal whether those running the prison education do it because they are required to or because they genuinely believe it is important to offer prisoners more skills.

Lesley, 17, at Styal, left school as soon as she could with no qualifications:

'That was why I got into shoplifting – because I couldn't see I'd be able to get a job. It was my personal officer who talked to me about what a difference it would make if I had literacy and numeracy skills. She explained how I might be able to train to work on computers and that sounded good. So I went to classes.'

Dropping out

The number of children excluded from school has risen sharply, from 3,000 in the early 1990s to around 10,400 by the end of the decade in England and Wales, and there is a well-established link between being out of school and offending. One study of persistent young offenders of all ages found that eight out of 10 of these had been excluded from school.[4]

The story of Jules, 17 when he was sent to Huntercombe, typifies the instability and disruption that is so often integral to the lives of excluded children who have turned to crime:

'I was ahead of my class in reading and writing when I was little because my Mum took my education seriously. She taught me before I even started school and she always did reading with me after school. Then when I was eight she put me into care – I don't know why but I suppose I must have been naughty. My Dad wouldn't have me 'cos he already had a wife and five other children. I didn't like my foster home and I started being trouble at school – showing off and that. They kicked me out of the foster home and school around the same time. I was put into a care home I really liked and I settled at school and was doing okay. But then the local authority said I shouldn't be their financial responsibility and I was moved again. This time I went to a family that really was hard on me. I was feeling very churned up inside all the time and I got into fights at school and I disrupted class. In time they excluded me.

'It was when I was out on the street with other excluded kids, some of them older, that I felt I'd found my family. They were good to me so when they wanted me to do crime with them of course I agreed. We did a lot of burglaries and shoplifting and I forgot all about school. It didn't have anything to offer.'

Getting back into education

Prison education was first contracted out to local colleges in 1992 with the emphasis on value for money – meaning that prisons were expected to go for the cheapest tender which, as several governors complained, meant they did not get best-quality teaching. At the same time subjects like art, drama and music were cut back. Since 1995 the emphasis of the prison core curriculum has been on literacy, numeracy, IT and social and life skills. At that time government made a commitment to reduce the number of prisoners released without basic skills at Level 2 or above. A fine idea in theory, but how effectively can basic educational provision be delivered to these difficult, resistant children one-fifth of whom have special educational needs? Few of the teachers working in prisons with juveniles and those YOs who choose to attend lessons have the qualifications and experience for this group, let alone special needs training or experience.[5]

Yet for all the disadvantages, prison should have a fairly good chance of getting young inmates who have been out of school back into education, with small classes and flexibility for individual needs, even though students may come by default, as Professor David Wilson at the University of Central England notes:

> 'You can't ignore the fact that they are physically captive, often bored, and prison education departments can be a welcome diversion or even a haven and refuge for those having a hard time. If teachers can capitalise on this and treat prisoners as individuals and with kindness they may be able to lead inmates to see that they can enjoy education.'

A prison frequently picked out for its creative and inspiring education department and where inmates too express a high level of satisfaction is Lancaster Farms. It offers subjects ranging from maths, English and information technology to family and community studies including parenting courses. The prison consistently achieves a high number of NVQ qualifications and has had a number of young men go on to university. But governor David Thomas says firmly: 'I am more proud of raising the basic level of literacy than of the odd lad who may go on to college or university although obviously they please me greatly.' But of course he has also come across plenty who are defensive about their lack of learning:

> 'I go to sit with some of the most difficult boys and ask why they aren't doing anything about the fact they can't read. I remember one so vividly saying, "I'm ashamed of it." When a young person says something like that it opens a door to talking about what has gone on in their lives. Then I can talk about how not having learnt to read is not surprising and they don't have to feel ashamed. But shame is what a great many feel and they go to great lengths to disguise it.'

It is a view shared by Chris Tchaikovsky, director of Women in Prison. It was during her time in Holloway as a young offender that she began studies which took her on to university where she did a degree in philosophy and remained out of prison from then on. So it is that WIP now goes into prisons and helps inmates who want to do distance learning courses, often in basic skills. But Tchaikovsky is well aware how carefully they have to tread with young women whose 'self-esteem is often through the floor'. She says:

> 'We don't talk about numeracy and literacy because they are school words and so many of the girls and women have had very bad experiences of school. We talk about word-power and number-power which suggest that the women themselves will be made stronger. Then we sit down and draw up an education plan. Someone says they want to be a lawyer and we say, "Right, let's start by getting some word-power and number-power under the belt." It is truly inspiring to watch them finding they can do these things and enjoy them. It is through the confidence gained that these girls and women look at how they just might be able to change their lives.'

Prisons that offer a broad and imaginative curriculum to pupils, including workshop-based subjects like car maintenance, engineering, photography, catering, drama, art and music, are more likely to attract and encourage inmates to stick to education. At Huntercombe, where they recognise how many young people would like to be able to work with music, Steive Butler, arts coordinator, wrote a course in music production and got it accredited. When Jules arrived at Huntercombe he was pulsing with rage and very resistant to the idea of 'more schooling'. But then he saw the high-tech music studio being built:

> 'I asked the person in charge if I could use the studio when it was ready and she said she would make a deal with me. If I did some literacy and numeracy then she'd get me into the studio. So I went to the education block and hung around a bit just watching. There were two nice women teachers and after a bit they suggested I join in. I liked them so I gave it a try. They really helped me, made me see I wasn't just a fool who had missed my chance to know anything. And they made me laugh with their jokes. So I stayed and got a couple of GCSEs at the end and I got a qualification in music production. Now I'm out I've been performing with a band that formed in prison and has Prince's Trust backing.'

Bruce, 20, serving life at Moorland for murder and with virtually no education when he arrived, was given individual teaching to study poetry and philosophy and work towards doing these at A level. At the other end of the scale catering is a favourite among children who have very little belief that they are capable of achieving anything. Lorraine Atkinson, who carried out research into prison education for the Howard League for Penal Reform, recalled the delight of a boy who made a curry and a pizza:

> 'Because it didn't feel like formal learning he enjoyed it, and of course there are plenty of ways an imaginative teacher can bring maths and reading into a catering class. In the same way with car maintenance they can point out to youngsters that if they want to work in a garage they will need to be able to prepare a bill for a customer.'

Where the system fails
There are, however, prisons where education is far from ideal. Lorraine Atkinson described to me how in too many YOIs inmates are given a printed worksheet and just expected to get on as best they can. Steve, 18, was one of several who remembers 'teaching' that was as good as useless. He was at Portland: 'Our teacher used to give us something to do then pick up his book and begin reading. If we interrupted to ask for help he was very cross. I don't think I learned anything there.'

The quality of teaching varies enormously. Some teachers find it dull and dispiriting work, some are too young and inexperienced and there is a high turnover because the pay is low. There are also always inmates who disrupt classes because they don't want to be there.

One of the commonest complaints from governors was that although the money for core skills learning – most significantly literacy and numeracy – was to be ring-fenced so that prisoners should get their s pecified number of hours, other subjects have to be funded out of their general budget and with year-on-year cuts imaginative workshops and subjects chosen by very few students tend to be casualties. Nor can many YOIs provide as much education as is wanted. In the new education block at Moorland I was told they could cater for only around 130 prisoners – about half the number of YOs usually housed in the institution at any one time.

Even when education is available prisoners talked to me about the attitude of officers in several prisons who do not see it as important. This can mean they are not bothered if a prisoner misses a lesson, they may fail to get them to evening classes or else they deliver them late. Guy, 18, who had been in a north country YOI, recollected one officer who said it straight: 'What's the point in spending taxpayers' money on educating you lot when you're just going to go out and offend again.'

Education can achieve only a very limited amount when inmates are on DTOs serving sentences of just a couple of months inside. A number of prison staff felt that practical workshop activities would probably be more effective for these young short-timers because it frequently takes time to get a juvenile to settle down before learning can begin in a classroom. This being so, the courts should think very hard about sending a child to prison for a few months if he or she is in school when sentenced, particularly if, as happens, it means their breaking off studies for examinations which it may not be possible to study for or sit inside. Equally, prisoners on longer sentences should not be moved around if they are working towards an examination without provision being made for them to continue these studies at the next prison they are moved to. Even then the move may be disruptive and damaging to their chances of doing well.

At best, then, lessons for YOs can get them back into education, persuade them to try something new and give them the opportunity to gain qualifications they would probably never have managed outside. But at worst it is a depressing waste of everyone's time. Governors blame lack of funding and budget cuts for the low morale of teachers, and in a prison where few subjects are on offer, there may be little to motivate the inmates. Given that of all aspects of the regime, education has the greatest potential to offer young people a way out of crime, thus saving the taxpayer a good deal of money, this seems a false economy indeed.

Physical education

At the mention of PE and especially time in the gym many prisoners' eyes light up. In Holloway three girls who had agreed to talk with me emerged from the swimming pool and were still damp, wrapped in towels, as we spoke. At Moorland they were celebrating the fact that a young man who had turned out to be an exceptionally good footballer, and who had been taken for a trial with a local professional football club, had been offered a three-year contract for when he was released.

It is easy to understand the appeal of PE. It is a way young inmates can use some of their pent-up energy and feel fitter. It is also a way that those who have never won success in academic education can achieve and do well, in the process improving their self-confidence. The head of PE at Moorland when I visited, had a strikingly inspiring approach to his work. He had seen how he could use his department to teach more than just physical exercise. He explained:

'When I arrived the PE department had just had a damning report and we were dealing with some very difficult prisoners. An analysis showed that more than 70% were violent and in some age-groups 100% were drug abusers. I set up a package of recreational activities and some basic education as part of the PE package. On induction the prisoners could choose what they wanted to do – weights, basketball, hockey, badminton, circuit training, gymnastics, running, yoga and so on. They were entitled to two hour-and-a-half sessions a week. The idea was to give them some autonomy in choosing what they would do. Then we added on coaching for vocational awards. We also introduced a first aid week and treating sports injuries – the kind of thing I would want my children to do.

'The way we got them to do some numeracy and literacy was by opening a small classroom attached to the gym. When they were there doing their sports, feeling good about themselves, it was possible to persuade them that it would really be a good idea to try some basic skills. Whereas many of them just refused to do education in classrooms.'

David Thomas, governor at Lancaster Farms, likewise explained how they use 'gentle coercion':

'A lot of kids say, we don't like school but we'll do PE. I say, well you can't read and write so you can't do PE unless you do a little bit of this and that. Because they very much want to do PE they agree. It surprises them that quite often begin to enjoy education as well as their exercise. But why on earth do they have to come to prison to learn that sport and education can both offer them something?'

Sadie, 16, at Styal for being involved in an attack on another girl whom she discovered with her boyfriend, had decided when she did badly at school that she could never succeed at education and so she dropped out:

'When I came here I told them straight they could put me in a class but I wouldn't learn. They couldn't make me. I went to PE because I'm good at sport. The teacher spoke to me about how I could perhaps go to college and train to be a PE instructor but that I'd need to read and write and understand numbers. I wasn't sure at first but it began to seem like they were offering me an opportunity to do something other than crime. Something I'd really enjoy. So I went to classes for literacy and all that and found it wasn't impossible to understand. And when I leave here I have a college place.'

The amount of exercise inmates are allowed varies considerably from prison to prison. Where there are well-equipped indoor sports facilities, as at Moorland and Holloway, there is no reason other than staff shortages why prisoners should not get their designated quota of at least two hours a week, up to one hour a day. But when prisons rely on outdoor facilities young inmates can be refused their time because of inclement weather. Nor is there any uniformity in quality of facilities at different YOIs. Sir David Ramsbotham inveighed against the badly maintained, inadequate sports grounds and the lack of any interest in making exercise constructive and demanding that he found in some YOIs. Given the emphasis put on exercise for mental and physical well-being by the world outside prison, it seems extraordinary that it is not a priority.

One inmate expressed just how important a good gym and PE can be for a young person who has few other skills when he filled in a form containing the question 'What is the Best Time of Day?' He replied: 'When we have jim.'

Offending behaviour courses

Even allowing for the hyperbole that comes easily to many young prisoners, when Sabrina, 17, at Holloway, described her crime to me it was easy to understand why she had been advised to do an anger management course:

> 'I assaulted a police officer … I broke his arm and stamped on him. Another time I had punched my head teacher and knocked her out. She called me a black fool. Yeah I've always been easy with my fists … and this is the way things have gone. But I hate it here and it's not worth being locked up. So I am going to anger management and all that shit to try to stop me losing my temper. I'll be able to test out how good it is because I keep losing my temper in here 'cos the other inmates they get right lippy.'

Living skills – the overall term for the courses designed to address offending behaviour and to teach young prisoners skills for coping in a different way – were introduced by the Prison Service in 1992. They are seen as an essential part of this government's emphasis on reducing offending and also to introduce offenders, who often give the person affected by their crime little heed, to the idea of empathy with victims. It startled one young man when his living skills tutor asked him how he would feel if someone had mugged his mother as he had a middle-aged woman: 'I said I knew I'd go mad, want to get my hands on the person what done it and show them how it feels. That was a shock because it really made me think the woman I threatened with a knife must have been very upset just like my Mum would be.'

The accredited courses currently being run for juvenile and older YOs are: Reasoning and Rehabilitation, Enhanced Thinking Skills, which includes anger management, and the Sex Offender Treatment Programme. The first two were developed in response to research which showed the need to target thinking and cognitive deficits, to show YOs how they can learn to think about their actions and choose to act differently. Although Thinking Skills are also offered in adult prisons most of the original research was carried out with YOs. The kind of situations used in the sessions are supposed to replicate those that adolescents might find themselves in and where they might offend. The Sex Offender Treatment Programme, designed for adults, may be adapted for younger prisoners. Reasoning and Reacting, a new cognitive skills course, is currently being piloted by the Prison Service. It is designed to get prisoners thinking about the ways they react in certain situations and to see how they might choose to react differently.

Justin, 19 when he was sent over to Huntercombe to finish a three-year term for armed robbery, arrived with lot of anger which he acted out much of the time:

> 'I used to be impatient, that was one of my downfalls and I could never concentrate for long periods of time. But the courses – anger management and reasoning skills – have taught me to stop and think about what is going on, not just react. I feel I've learned to take constructive criticism. If I disagree with someone I'm able to tell them without swearing, raving, ranting.'

Money for the accredited courses, which are a key part of the government's drive to be proactive in confronting prisoners with their offending behaviour, has been ring-fenced by the Prison Service for all prisoners. There is also some dedicated training for prison officers who will deliver the courses, and psychologists have input into the content and may well be involved in overseeing them. The Home Office accredits, trains and monitors the courses using an external panel of academics. Videoing of sessions has been used to assess how well they are conducted and how effective they are with prisoners and in some cases those delivering the courses have been instructed to rethink how they will run them so that they engage inmates' interest.

At Lancaster Farms governor David Thomas and his team developed their own short course on crime and its consequences, lasting three days. He describes it:

> 'On the first day we address the crimes the prisoners have committed and their reactions to them. They very often see themselves as victims. Their line is: "I'm in prison and they are not." If it is a burglary they assume the victim is insured so that is okay. The point is to let them say what they feel and to have it heard, then when we get down to discussing how they had a choice and the victim didn't, you often see a change. Then we get them to think about whether that is how they want to go on and how they might find a different way to live their lives. The idea all the way through is to put responsibility onto the individual, trying to get them to accept that no matter how tough their

life has been and how much they are entitled to understanding and sympathy for that, in the end they have to take responsibility for choosing to commit a crime. We attempt to measure effectiveness by doing an entrance and exit assessment to see if there has been a change of attitude. We have seen more victim empathy afterwards, but if you did another assessment after six months, who knows?'

At Styal senior psychologist Mike Jennings runs a number of courses using role-playing. He explains:

'It is quite powerful. We used to have a simple scenario where each of the inmates had to pretend to be someone who had a crime committed against them. The effect was amazing. All the old catchphrases like "they'll get it back on insurance", "it didn't really hurt them", "they shouldn't have got in my way", had gone. They really started talking about the victim, but it is then important that they have thought things through so that it becomes part of their conscious thinking, because that is what they will have to draw on in future situations. In another session we used an example of a man and a woman going out and getting drunk. She hits him, he restrains her and we question how far he is entitled to use restraint. The idea is to get those doing the course thinking beyond their usual way and to help them develop ways to persuade someone else of their argument.'

Courses are not mandatory but there are incentives for those who choose to do them. Yet not everybody gets the opportunity, partly because of their high cost and partly because there may not be staff available who are capable of delivering them. There is considerable discrepancy in the number of courses delivered in different prisons, although of course this may have something to do with how many prisoners require them.

Plenty of prison staff talked about the value of these courses which often include role play, and they are generally liked by offenders although inevitably there are a number who resist the very idea or declare they were, in the words of one, 'complete bollocks'. Reconviction data is at an early stage but it has been seen to be promising in the case of adults who have completed offending behaviour courses.

Jules, 17, at Huntercombe, is equivocal about how much the courses he attended have helped:

'I went to behavioural stuff – anger management, victim empathy. I quite liked them and I understood what they were trying to do with me ... Trouble is I know there's a victim when I'm committing a crime, I know somebody will feel something, but I'm not bothered at the time because I'm doing it for the money or whatever I'm getting out of it.

I'd like to say I would feel differently next time but I'm not convinced I've changed that much.'

For Michelle, 17, at Holloway the courses got her thinking:

'I found myself thinking about things that had never crossed my mind before because I did everything on autopilot ... I think about victims more now. But most of all the courses made me think about what I became when I was on heroin. I was shooting up every day and committing crime – a lot of shoplifting – to get the money. My being an addict split my Mum and stepdad up. Now I know I just want to get out and keep out of trouble.'

Drugs

Doug's story illustrates well the relief and release from misery and seemingly insoluble problems that many YOs describe as the reason they become addicted to drugs:

'My mother died when I was 12 but my Dad quickly remarried and I didn't get on with my stepmother. I put myself into care and my brother stopped talking to me. It was a lot to go through at the time and I began smoking pot when I was 14 and at 16 I went on to speed for a few months. I had got engaged and we had plans. I stopped using drugs but then she died when I was 18 and I started using smack because it dulled the pain down. That was when my offences began. I was doing burglary to fund my £150-a-day habit. They sent me to prison when I broke into a chemist's store to get some drugs I wanted to help me come off. I threatened the chemist himself with a syringe full of blood. I can understand that the courts take threatening someone with AIDS seriously so I wasn't surprised to be sent down.'

There is no absolute figure on how many children and young people go into prison addicted, but most governors I spoke with thought it was at least three-quarters of their intake. A recent study found one in three sentenced female YOs and one in six sentenced males are on or addicted to drugs.[6] Some 76% of young women and 91% of young men reported to Sir David Ramsbotham and his team in 1997 that they had used drugs at some time.[7] A survey in 1998–9 showed that for juveniles, drug use over the previous year was the strongest predictor of serious or persistent offending.[8] It meant they were considerably more likely than non-drug users to offend often to support drug habits costing hundreds of pounds per week, and of course young people using drugs are frequently unable to find or hold down jobs.

The scale and severity of the drug culture and its link with crime has made getting YOs clean a priority for the government. In April 1999 they gave £76 million for drug services inside prison for all prisoners, the bulk of this earmarked for Category A drugs. In 1995 Mandatory Drug Testing (MDT) was introduced throughout all prisons. Random urine tests – 'taking the piss' as inmates refer to it – are now used, as well as searches and sniffer dogs, to detect illegal drugs. The success of MDT is measured by the number of positive tests done on prisoners over a period of time and these have reduced beyond the government's own target. But prison ethnographer Anita Wilson warns that there are flaws in this measure: 'MDT has simply pushed prisoners onto Category A drugs because they are eliminated from the bloodstream within 48 hours whereas cannabis remains for days. So prisoners take hard drugs on a Friday night knowing they are very unlikely to be tested before Tuesday.' Campaigners also criticise the high cost of MDT when the money could be far better spent on helping prisoners deal with their addictions. There was talk too of how MDT had led to an increase in tension and resentment among staff, as well as to a black market in clean substitute urine samples.

Young prisoners also spoke of how drugs were available in their prisons and how, if you really wanted a particular drug, you might well find an officer willing to supply it 'if he likes you or the price is right', although even the most open of staff I spoke to thought this would be a very rare occurrence. Most governors insisted that although some drugs got through in the nappies of prisoners' babies, in gifts and through things like kissing, they were sure they did not have a big drug problem. Chris Tchaikovsky, director of Women in Prison, laughs at what she calls blind naivety: 'I walk around a prison with the governor saying everyone is clean and then I look around and see these girls with their gleaming eyes and other-world expressions completely off their trollies.'

Certainly governors appeared universally to prioritise getting addicted inmates clean. David Lancaster, governor at Holloway, sees this as offering them something: 'I've never met one who didn't crave help with breaking the cycle. We don't force anyone into detox but they ask for it over and over because they see what a mess drugs are making of their lives.'

Hazel Jackson, in charge of the former YO unit at Holloway, talked of how they dealt with a situation where some 55% of their young women went through detox. Methadone was used for heroin users but a high proportion were on a cocktail of legal drugs such as anti-depressants and tranquillisers and illegal substances, so that they needed help in stopping altogether and coping with that. Not that they always appreciated it, said Jackson:

'A heroin addict was brought in the other day and she was determined not to cooperate with us. She lost a stone, going down from seven to six, during her detox. Her parents came to see her and afterwards she collapsed. But a few days later she was a different person. She had begun eating as she felt better and she had put on weight, her face had filled out and she was talking coherently. I do believe we saved her life.'

Katy, 17, in Holloway for 'a lot of robbery' which she committed to feed her heroin habit, is one of the young women who went through the prison's programme: 'I couldn't have decided to stop by myself. I was screaming for the stuff when I couldn't get it. They put me on methadone here, even so it was hard – really hard – but I've got clean and I don't long for drugs any more. I just hope I can stay that way outside.'

Recognising how difficult it was for detoxed prisoners to go 'whoosh back on to the wing', in Jackson's words, a post-detox unit was set up at Holloway where inmates can spend some days re-orienting. And in this prison, as in some others, drug workers are brought in from outside agencies to work with prisoners during their sentence but also when they leave.

Over the next three years, £41 million of the money designated for beating drugs in prison is being used on detoxification and rehabilitation programmes: 23 different types of programme are being developed and to date these operate in 10 YOIs. However, few prisons have detox units like the one that was set up at Holloway; instead prisoners are offered visits by CARATs (counselling, advice, referrral, assessment, throughcare) workers who are now employed to come into prisons from community agencies.[9]

Methadone is not used in all YOIs and David Thomas, governor at Lancaster Farms, finds his inmates often prefer to cold turkey by themselves. The important thing, he says, is that they are supported through this time. Bill, 20, who spent six months at Dorchester as one of a very few YOs, remembers coming off by himself:

'I wanted to know I had the strength to do it because that's what you need outside. It's no good if you are dependent on somebody helping you do it. My aim was to be able to go home and know if I slipped and began using again I was able to stop. But it helped doing it in prison because I couldn't get drugs so I couldn't fail.'

Deliver these standards

Martin Narey, Director General of the Prison Service, has talked enthusiastically of his hope for the youth justice reforms, calling them 'a commitment to make custody a positive and purposeful experience' and claiming that the Prison Service has listened to the criticisms made by Sir David Ramsbotham and is working to make improvements.

This chapter has focused on what is positive while acknowledging that even the best of prisons have their problems and there are improvements to be made. The least satisfactory situation is that of older YOs who are in real danger of becoming a twilight zone unless the Prison Service thinks seriously about the needs of this group now they are separated off from the juveniles. The complaint frequently made to me by staff working with 18–21 year olds is that money is now directed to the juvenile estate and consequently less is available for older YOs, even though the needs of disturbed young people do not simply disappear when they reach 18. Paul McDowell, deputy governor at Feltham, told me how the high investment in Feltham's new, custom-built juvenile wing had showed up just how little the older YOs receive of the resources necessary to provide a positive regime. Despite this, by the end of 2001 he reported:

'Having worked hard to create a new juvenile unit that has been praised, we have now focused on the older YOs and increased activity for them over the past year … Barry Denton was brought in specifically to work on improving conditions for the older YOs and not only are we pleased with the progress, but it has been praised by Martin Narey.'

Perhaps older YOs do not need quite the same degree of child-centred care as the juveniles, although Juliet Lyon, director of the Prison Reform Trust, believes the conditions of the Children Act should still apply to them. This age-group certainly needs caring for; older YOs require stimulating and demanding activities and time out of cell just as the younger prisoners do. The fear is that without sufficient facilities or funding these still impressionable and vulnerable young people will be integrated into the adult prisoner population, with no recognition of their need for a different kind of treatment.

All YOIs must have continuous adequate resourcing if the good practice of such prisons as Huntercombe and Lancaster Farms – which do show signs of achieving lower reoffending rates – is to be maintained and replicated in other institutions across the country. But governors talked to me despairingly of the year-on-year cuts they have to make to their budgets even though prison intakes are rising. Sir David Ramsbotham told me stoutly that, although it was clear that the quality of regimes was being eroded by cost reduction, he was optimistic about the impressive work being done in some YOIs: 'We have shown that those standards are deliverable.'

NOTES

1. Information supplied by HM Prison Service press office, October 2001.
2. HM Prison Service, *Annual Report and Accounts 1999–2000*; Paul McDowell, deputy governor of Feltham YOI, November 2001.
3. Joe Levenson, *Monitoring Prison Regimes*. London, Prison Reform Trust, 1999–2000.
4. T. Martin, C. Hayden, D. Turner and K. Ramsell, *Out of School and Into Trouble?*

Exclusion from school and persistent young offenders. University of Portsmouth/Hampshire Constabulary, 1999.

5. *Missing the Grade: Education for children in prison.* London, Howard League for Penal Reform, July 2001.
6. *Young Offenders: Facts and Figures.* London, Prison Reform Trust, 2001.
7. *Young Prisoners: A thematic review by HM Chief Inspector of Prisons for England and Wales.* London, Home Office, 1997.
8. C. Flood-Page *et al.*, *Findings from the 1998/99 Youth Lifestyles Survey.* London, Home Office Research, Development and Statistics Directorate, 2000.
9. Information from the Prison Service Directorate of Resettlement, London, 2001.

'I believe women have a substantially different criminal profile to men – when we compare the crimes of women prisoners to the crimes of male prisoners we are not comparing like with like. The figures reveal that the more serious the crimes committed the greater the difference between men and women and we need to acknowledge this.'

Chris Tchaikovsky, director of Women in Prison

7 A sex apart?

Tola, 17, sitting next to me in the association area on the Holloway YO Unit, gives a big, crooked smile:

'Naive or what, wasn't I? I thought nobody saw me slip these fancy briefs and bra into my bag but then there was this big fat hand on my shoulder. Tried to do a runner but no chance. It was my second conviction for shoplifting and the magistrate said I needed to learn that was no way to "meet my desires in life". I got three months which isn't so bad except I've lost my flat and they don't want me at home, and my boyfriend's gone off with another girl so life doesn't look too good right now.'

The thing Shane, 19, found most painful in prison was seeing the women with their babies. A single mother, she had a three year old son when she was sentenced to nine months for drug offences. The boy's grandmother got custody while Shane served her time, but when she came out the boy screamed when she tried to take him home and she hit him. 'My Mum, she said, I wasn't fit to look after the boy and she applied to keep custody. The courts gave it and that upset me so much I started on the drugs again – I'd detoxed in prison. I see Jesse at my Mum's house but I don't know how I'd look after him now with the drugs and I don't have a job – how do you get one with a criminal record like mine?'

Tola and Shane are typical of many of the girls and young women who end up behind bars. The crimes they have committed and their personal problems could almost certainly have been better addressed with community projects, secure housing and some constructive adult support. Instead their lives have been made measurably worse by time inside and it is not difficult to imagine that both may reoffend. Their prison sentences are also typical of the increasingly harsh way the courts are dealing with young women who transgress. In the decade from 1990 to 2000 the number of under-21 year old females sent to prison rose from 381 a year to 1,236.[1] But why should this be, given that there is little evidence to suggest that young women are becoming more deviant and threatening to society? The answer would seem to lie in the public's perception of young females as a growing menace, a threat, the tough stuff of, for example, the vastly popular TV series *Bad Girls*.

A perception of violence

This perception is strengthened by the prominence given by the media to particularly disturbing and vicious crimes committed by young women. Take the case of 18 year old Claire Marsh, found guilty of rape after she ripped the clothes off a woman whom she and a group of youths had persuaded onto a towpath, held her down and then stood laughing while a boy and an 18 year old man, also later convicted and imprisoned, raped the woman. Hers was a hideous crime, without doubt, but surely not worse than that of the males; yet the coverage focused almost entirely on Marsh, presumably because of her gender. A cluster of equally violent crimes committed by girls and young women between 1997 and 2000 was given enough press attention to create the impression that female violence is a terrifying phenomenon which requires the toughest measures to check it.

In fact such cases receive disproportionate coverage precisely because they are so rare. Media reporting dwells on the titillating idea of 'girlie gangs' and 'bad girls' and tends not to be interested in the altogether less sensational truth which shows just how few girls and young women ever commit crimes that are a physical threat to us. Consider: in 2000 just 241 girls under 21– and that included 100 juveniles – were sent to prison in England and Wales for crimes of violence against the person, out of a total of 1,236 young women. When this is compared with 3,302 males of the same age range – including 921 juveniles – sent to prison for violent crimes, out of a total of 20,086 young men, it becomes clear where the real risk lies.[2]

Many of the girls and young women I spoke with had no qualms about committing 'soft' crimes but felt strongly about not using violence while doing so. Christa, 18, in Styal for repeated shoplifting, gave voice to this view: 'It's a different league of crime isn't it? I'm not someone who could slash another person. And if I killed someone I don't know how I'd live with myself. No, for me just getting the gear is the point. I don't feel bad about that because I know the sort of people I rob will get it back from insurance.'

Bella, 17, in Holloway for burglary, had her own morality too: 'I've nicked a lot in my time but I have my standards. I'd never steal from an old person or someone disabled and I've never hurt anyone. I'm quite proud of that.'

Yet however small the actual threat posed by young women, there has been a rise in the amount of violent crime they commit. Where, in 1990, 58 girls and young women under 21 were imprisoned for violent crimes, the figure of 241 a decade later suggests that some young women are becoming more willing to use violence.[3]

The idea that we must fear the female footfall behind us in the street, or the girl we can better imagine in a disco dressed in trendy garb pulling a knife on us, is new. But when girls and young women, in whatever number, commit truly dangerous and violent offences they cannot be ignored. If they pose a threat to the safety of others then, just as much as boys, they need to be removed from society. Girls like Marsha, 17, in Holloway. She is serving a long sentence for armed robbery where knives and guns were used, causing grievous bodily harm to victims. Talking to me she stood there arms akimbo, a tough-guy expression on her face, as she related how she had been in prison before for ABH – beating up a girl who was 'getting too lippy on the street' – and for an offence she wouldn't describe committed with a group of males.

Gina, 17, in Holloway for the latest of several violent offences, willingly talks about taking pride in being seen as 'wild':

'I have used a knife to cut someone after I'd had a few drinks. This girl, she looked at me funny and I didn't like it. And I've been cut in fights when I was angry enough I could have stabbed the other person. This time I'm here for GBH. I don't like being in prison but it probably won't stop me because I think I need to be seen as tough. It's not good being a pussy in this world.'

But why should more girls and young women be resorting to violence – even if their numbers are small in real terms? Chris Tchaikovsky puts forward this view:

'These girls and young women see that there is a choice between joining the "Anybodies", as the women were known in West Side Story, who might be high-spirited but ultimately conformed to society's traditional ideas on how women should live their lives, or of becoming a tomboy, a different type of female, and identifying with males. Young women see how men hold the power and it may well seem that their lives, including their criminal behaviour, are more interesting and excitingly dangerous than the depressing passivity and acceptance of the Anybodies.'

This tallies with Sir David Ramsbotham's view that: 'Young women in custody are by definition unusual. They diverge from the vast majority of their peers in resisting the powerful pressures in society for women to conform to gender rules. Their behaviour attracts stigma because it does not fit widely held images of womanhood.'[4]

Mike Jennings, senior psychologist at Styal, has seen plenty of examples of girls and young women who have been passive for years and then suddenly snapped:

> 'The women have very often put up with dreadful treatment and turned the anguish they felt on themselves. Then one day their desperation turns to anger and they unleash all their pent-up feelings in an act of violence. But you can't imagine it when you see them here afterwards, they are so often distraught at what they have done. Whereas male rage may remain and may even make young men feel they were justified, the young women we see here are much more likely to hate themselves.'

The other familiar cause of girls' and young women's violence is sexual jealousy, which had led several young inmates I talked with to commit GBH against their perceived rival. In these reactions we may be seeing an influence from popular culture – films, Lara Croft-style computer games and comic strips – where feisty young women do not passively accept their fate but fight back, hard and dirty if need be. Lisa, 19, in Holloway for five years, tells:

> 'I got into an argument with a girl friend and I ended up going for her with a knife, cutting her up. I didn't plan it but where I am from – the Seven Sisters Road near here – you have to protect yourself so I have carried a knife since I was 12. I just flipped when this girl came on strong with my boyfriend. I felt as though the one person I thought was there for me was being taken... My mother threw me out just before I was 13 and I went into care. I never met my Dad.'

An officer at Holloway, a confidante of several of her young charges, thinks it hardly surprising that the young women she sees, who have so rarely been given emotional care or security in their lives, become ferocious if they feel a relationship which appears to offer them these things is under threat.

Female violence can be as impulsive and random as that of males when drugs are involved as, increasingly, they appear to be. Kate, 17, serving time in Holloway, is typical:

'I started taking drugs when I just got into my teens. I was miserable and they helped and because I wasn't using much nobody at home noticed. But then someone asked me if I wanted heroin and I was curious. I was also sure it wouldn't get me but it did and then I never had enough money for my needs. I lived on the edge, shoplifting to support a £160-a-day habit. When I first used I was really high and buzzy and I was in this state when I got into a fight in a pub with another girl. I hit her with a bottle and it broke. Yes, she was hurt quite bad.'

Tougher on females

The perception that young women are enough of a risk to need taking out of circulation appears to be affecting sentencing. Several campaigning organisations assert that young women are being given harsher sentences than in the past. It is something Juliet Lyon, director of the Prison Reform Trust, describes as 'an issue of injustice that needs tackling', while Fran Russell, assistant director at the Howard League for Penal Reform, points to the League's finding of a 175% rise in the number of 15–17 year old girls sent to prison between 1992 and 1996 – more than two and a half times the percentage increase in the prison population as a whole. She says: 'We suspect that magistrates and judges are being influenced by the drip feed of stories of "girl gangs" and "girl violence" and that some are handing down custodial sentences to teenage girls who previously would have received a non-custodial sentence.'

Young women are more likely than young men to be imprisoned for first offences.[5] The other discrimination girls face is being imprisoned for crimes which might not put a male inside. Because certain behaviour, such as pub brawling and punch-ups on the street, is seen as classic male conduct it is often taken more seriously when young women behave this way.[6] Nor is that the only potentially harmful inequality for young women. For whereas, after the division of juveniles and older YOs, male prisons were given more than £50 million to be spent on setting up constructive regimes and conditions recognising the needs of children, female prisons received virtually nothing for juvenile girls. David Lancaster, governor at Holloway, explains angrily:

'We were expected to meet the higher standards to work with juveniles on DTOs and on top of everything we were getting a far greater number than we had been led to believe we would. We already had staffing difficulties and the work with juveniles is, necessarily, very staff-intensive. What we found was that delivering the regime required for juveniles was done at a cost to what we could do for older youngsters.'

The not altogether satisfactory result at Holloway was that in the summer of 2001 the YO unit that had been set up in 1998 to house young women apart from adult prisoners was closed. This was because Holloway was considered to be overstretched in coping with so many different types of female prisoner and that juveniles and older YOs would be better catered for elsewhere. Although Holloway does still receive a few younger prisoners, usually on remand or waiting to be sent to other prisons. Before its closure the YO unit had won considerable praise for its specially selected staff, who had a high level of commitment to working with young women, and for having successfully brought together people from different agencies to work as a team. I heard very positive comments from inmates about the way they were treated there, the constructive help given, the sense of security they felt – as well, of course, as their discontents. It is to be hoped that the new arrangements, which will mean juveniles being sent to dedicated sites around the country that will receive Youth Justice Board money, succeed in matching the best of what the Holloway unit offered.

Getting children out of prison

Organisations campaigning to have children under 18 years removed from prison consider it even more imperative for girls than for boys. The number of girls given custodial sentences is so small that very little provision has been created especially for them. This means they frequently end up a long way from home, which can make it difficult for families to visit and maintain all-important links. Also, they may not receive the full regime or education programmes that boys are offered, and so may spend more hours shut up in their cells, or in the words of one teenager, 'getting a very limited choice of subjects to study or things to do'.

Historically, the most serious impact of this lack of provision has been that under-18 year old girls were held alongside adults in adult prisons, even though this contravened the UN Convention on the Rights of the Child. In 1997 the Howard League for Penal Reform brought a test case citing a 16 year old girl held in Risley prison alongside adult prisoners in conditions they considered grimly unsuitable and where there was no particular provision or facilities for older YOs or juveniles. The court ruled that it was unlawful for YOs under 21 – of either sex – to be in the same prison unit as adults and that they must be separated.[7]

This ruling was not accepted by the Conservative government. Though the Thatcher government had ratified the UN Convention in 1991, it derogated from the article which stated that children should not be put into adult institutions. So YOs continued to be imprisoned alongside adults. Soon after the Labour government came to power in 1997 Jack Straw promised that juvenile girls (under 18) would be removed from prison and put into secure accommodation. By the beginning of 2001 this had not happened. However, since the introduction of the juvenile estate, all juveniles and YOs are separated at reception and go on to separate wings and it is only in the mother and baby units that under-18s spend time with older women – because the Prison Service does not have the resources to provide separate facilities for them.

A commitment was made in the Crime and Disorder Act 1998 to make 15–16 year old girls and vulnerable boys a priority for places in secure accommodation when they are given custodial sentences, and 17 year olds should follow as more places become available. This was agreed in principle by Jack Straw in 2000. However the obstacle here is that there are still not enough such places and so some juvenile girls remain within the prison system.

Prison is not designed for girls and young women

Because the criminal justice system has to provide for vastly more males than females, the women tend to be slotted into the male prison model regardless of their different practical and psychological requirements.[8] This means that all too often women receive education, offending behaviour programmes and detox programmes designed for male prisoners and which take no account of the particular needs of girls and young women. In the view of prison ethnographer Anita Wilson:

> 'An awareness of the difference between young women's and young men's lives is essential when treatments and programmes are planned for them. Take education for example. A girl or young woman in prison may have looked after family members or even a child of her own, she may have had a very different approach to education in school to a male peer and young women may well have a different take on life. All these things affect how they might be brought into education and how it might be made appropriate to them. And this is even clearer in the case of offending behaviour courses.
>
> 'A very high percentage of girls and young women have suffered abuse and this links to their misuse and abuse of drugs and alcohol. It also gives them a marked tendency to choose inappropriate relationships which reinforce their sense of vulnerability. All this should be acknowledged in programmes for them but of course it's not if those programmes were not designed with them in mind.'

Wilson, who was one of the team that developed the original Trust for the Study of Adolescence training pack for staff working with YOs, is now adapting the programme to meet the specific needs of women.

Girls and young women in prison very often have even higher levels of emotional distress and psychiatric morbidity than boys and young men.

A 1997 study found that one in five of all women prisoners had spent time as an in-patient in a mental hospital or psychiatric ward and as many as 40% reported receiving help or treatment for some kind of mental health problem in the year before coming into prison.[9] For many these problems dated from childhood and adolescence and appeared to contribute to their offending behaviour and increase their vulnerability to self-harm. The Chief Inspector of Prisons' thematic review of young prisoners in the same year reported that 37% of young women claimed they had attempted suicide before coming to prison, compared with 7% of young men, while 15% said they had self-harmed. Almost half said they had been sexually abused.[10]

Tilly, 17, describes how her father sexually abused her from a very young age:

> 'I used to wake up and hear him pushing open the door, usually in the middle of the night when Mum was asleep, or when she was out shopping. He did it to my sister too. We never said anything because he once told us how the father of a girl dropped her into the canal one night after she told on him, and everyone believed she had committed suicide. I couldn't wait to get away from home so the first man who wanted me seemed like God. He was a bit older and I was very happy when he suggested we move in together. But then he started beating me about and wanting a lot of odd sexual stuff – specially after I'd told him about my Dad. I was miserable but I didn't know what I'd do if I left him and in a way it was a relief when he offered me drugs because they blotted everything out. But then I was hooked and he didn't give me enough gear for what I needed so I had to get some myself … that's why I got in with some others doing burglary.'

The babies are punished too

When girls and young women who are pregnant or already mothers are given a custodial sentence their children also pay the price. Either they must spend their early formative years in a prison environment or they must be separated from their mothers with all the damage that can cause. Given that a high proportion of women who are imprisoned have given birth during their teens compared with the general population, the government and courts should consider how they might deal with young mothers, many of whom rarely pose any real risk to society but who could almost certainly be better prepared for life as a parent in the community than in prison.

When pregnant girls and young women or those with very young children are imprisoned they may be offered a place on one of the four mother and baby units in England and Wales. In Holloway a mother and baby unit has been set up where young and older women mix, because there are not the resources to separate them, but the young women I talked to there generally expressed satisfaction with the 'orderly' way it was run and the kindness of staff in helping them to care for their babies.

In a welcoming room, the walls decorated with nursery-style pictures and baby and toddler toys at hand, the staff officer breaks off an animated conversation with a young woman, promising to return. She takes me to meet Bella, 17, who has a tiny baby draped over her shoulder. She was pregnant when she arrived with a 12-month sentence to serve. She was shocked to be sent to prison but says now:

> 'I didn't want to have my baby in prison. I cried and cried when I got here but I have to say they were kind to me from the beginning and made sure I looked after myself until the birth. My baby's four months old now and they've helped me a lot here. There are some good people who really like babies. We're encouraged to be with them a lot of the time so that we really experience what it will mean to be a mother when we are outside. We learn about nutrition and some child development stuff and I don't know I'd have got that on the outside. But still it's prison and I can't look after my baby just as I'd choose, I can't take her into the outdoors and she can't bond with her Dad in these early months which is bad. But I've got used to being here and knowing there are people who will help me, even though there are some who are right thugs and make life difficult. I just wish I could have had the good bits of the mother and baby unit on the outside because I think it's going to be hard to leave, hard to settle into a different routine with my new baby and I don't know yet where I'm going to go because my brother and I were adopted when we were little but it didn't work out well, I don't have a home with those parents now.'

Jackie, 17, who is now out of Holloway where she spent time with her baby, was less enthusiastic:

> 'They're not unkind but they have their ideas on how you should treat your kid and how your kid should behave, and that can be really hard. I've come up across officers on the mother and baby unit who thought I was a crap mother. It was really clear what they thought and that upsets you a lot. At least if you are on the wing you can be who you are and that's accepted. With a baby it's like they feel they're taking on responsibility for how your kid turns out.'

The mother and baby unit I visited at Styal was not as stimulating as Holloway but there was a kindly atmosphere with staff who gave the impression of seeing their young inmates as in need of mothering themselves. It was also clear from what several girls said that prisoners who got places there were considered to have 'a jammy deal'.

There are just 60 places on mother and baby units and each application for a place is chosen on merit. When a woman is given a place she will be allowed to have her child for a maximum of 18 months, and sometimes just nine months. Girls and young women with children who end up in custody are frequently sole carers, so if there is no relative willing or able to take on their children they may be put into care. Two women prisoners brought an action in 2000 claiming that the Prison Service's policy of removing children at a specific date was unlawful under the Children Act 1989 and the Human Rights Act 1998, but this failed.

Hazel Jackson, in charge of the YOs at Holloway, explains that:

'There are times when we have to refuse a woman a place on the mother and baby unit, or when it is not possible for a mother to keep a baby there because we fear she is too great a risk to other mothers and their children. We are well aware how cruel it can seem to people outside and we do get flak for decisions not to let someone come, but there are women whose crimes have been against children, who have personality disorders which make them dangerous, and just think what the public would say if we let a woman harm someone else's child. It wouldn't be right to take that risk.'

Nevertheless it is not difficult to imagine the distress for young women who have their children taken from them after spending months mothering them in circumstances that, ironically, may make bonding easier than it would have been outside. An officer at Styal describes it:

'I have sometimes had to take a child from a mother. I am sleepless for nights before the day comes because I'm a mother myself and I just think it's so wrong. Not surprisingly the mothers go mad. I've been hit, had abuse screamed at me – everything – when I've had to take these little kids who don't understand what is happening and then they are crying and shouting for their mothers. So many of these young women have never really had anyone whose love they felt they could trust and when they lose their child they go into dreadful depression or they self-harm. I just think it's the cruellest system.'

However far from ideal a prison environment may be for young children, some reformers argue that more places should be available on mother and baby units and that they should be able to cater for older children so that girls and young mothers (as well as older women) should not be separated from their children. The importance of early bonding is well recognised, as is the psychological damage that may be caused by separating a child of 18 months from their primary carer. The counter-argument, equally passionately held, is that if additional places are created on such mother and baby units, judges may be encouraged to send more children to prison with their mothers and that, given the tiny percentage of mothers who are incarcerated for offences that represent any kind of threat to society, reforms should instead focus on keeping mothers and their children out of prison.

Hazel Jackson agrees:

> 'Women coming here are upset, they often have multiple problems and they are very needy. I think we do the best we can under the circumstances but it's so far from ideal as the environment in which to mother a child. I see it as a failure of the courts that they can't find a better way. I wish an alternative to prison could be found – say residential houses in the community where mothers could be required to do some community service as their punishment but they could also be with their babies throughout their sentence.'

A better solution is needed

What we need to realise, says Chris Tchaikovsky at Women in Prison, where they work with young women on release, is that: 'We lock them up and send them out less not more able to cope, more not less angry and more likely to be violent. This way we feed the prisons of the future.'

Given the low level of risk they pose and the potential damage done by imprisoning girls and young women, there is surely a strong case for keeping them out of prison as much as possible and for using less expensive community punishments instead – ideally with counselling and support to deal with the problems that so often underlie their offending. In the particular case of mothers with children, childcare education could be built into the hours they are required to serve. This way they would pay for their offences but also be gaining skills that would help them to care for their child, while also maintaining the links with family and friends that are so often vital for a young mother.

This approach certainly worked for Natalie, 16, whose pale face, framed with long blonde hair, was transformed by a sudden smile when she told how she had been helped by the Portsmouth Community Safety Partnerships project which works with young people at risk of entering the criminal justice system. Aged 13, she had been put into care by her mother and expelled from school for getting into fights. She began thieving and selling her 'loot'. She also began drinking a lot:

> 'I didn't think about what was happening in my life. I just felt bad. I was introduced to heroin and got addicted, then my drug dealer

boyfriend got me pregnant but he didn't stick around. Things got diffi-cult with a friend and I ended up charged with ABH. I'd have been sent to prison but the Portsmouth set-up helped me by getting me on to activities they ran, finding me a mentor who taught me horse riding. She helped me kick drink and drugs so when I went to court they accepted that it would undo the good work that had been done if they put me in prison. But I'm the only one from my group who hasn't been in prison and I've given up crime. They haven't.'

NOTES

1. *Prison Statistics, England and Wales.* London, Home Office, 1990–2000.
2. *Ibid.*
3. *Ibid.*
4. *Young Prisoners: A thematic review by HM Chief Inspector of Prisons for England and Wales.* London, Home Office, 1997.
5. *Lost Inside – The imprisonment of teenage girls: Report of the Howard League Inquiry into the use of prison custody for girls aged under 18.* London, Howard League for Penal Reform, 1997.
6. Dr Loraine Geltsthorpe, Lecturer at the Institute of Criminology, University of Cambridge, in *The Guardian*, 15 August 2000.
7. The Flood ruling, 1997.
8. Dorothy Wedderburn, *Justice for Women.* London, Prison Reform Trust, 2000.
9. Nicola Singleton *et al.*, *Psychiatric Morbidity among Prisoners in England and Wales.* London, Office for National Statistics, 1997.
10. See note 4.

'They come out feeling dirty. They're given the prison issue bag with HMP stamped on it and if they have to catch a train they feel people are drawing away from them. They may have been Mr Big inside but so often they've got nothing on the outside and no idea how to cope. For months or even years they've been told when to go to bed, when to get up, what they must do at any time, what they must eat. And all too often the experience is dehumanising. They're called "you", pointed at, searched several times a day when they move from wing to wing. What kind of preparation is that for living a decent life outside?'

Ian Ross, director of Outside Chance

8 Freedom – or is it?

'I was in Bulwood Hall for attempted murder – four years. There was no preparation for coping, for knowing how I would go on from that moment when I stepped outside. It was scary. I didn't realise how dependent I had become on having all those rules so I didn't have to think for myself and the big world had changed … money, clothes, the attitude of people … seemed more horrible than when I went in.' Liz, 20.

Young people in prison almost always focus on their release date, dreaming of how it will be, comparing with others, competing in the grandiosity of their fantasies about what they will do when first outside. The release date becomes the thing around which they shape their time inside and cope with it, the day when they see themselves getting their lives back. Lying in their cells, visualising getting cosy with girl- or boyfriends, having a drink with mates down the pub, being free to walk the streets, travel where they want, these young people have a picture of life outside that takes little if any account of the impact prison will have had on their lives.

Dreams and reality can be very different and not surprisingly the transition from being an inmate within the prison system to stepping outside, the prison gate clanging behind them, and realising they are on their own, is not always so simple. John Harding, former director of the Inner London Probation Service, understands very well how difficult the transition from inside to outside may be:

'When you put youngsters into custody you freeze time, reality is suspended and so they adapt to the culture and that becomes their life.

When they come out they suddenly have to get to grips with reality again and they are faced with all the questions that are hard enough if you haven't been to prison: how am I going to gain money legitimately? How am I going to find accommodation? How am I going to restore a difficult relationship with a parent? How am I going to keep away from delinquent peers who helped me get into trouble in the first place?'

Jeannie, 17, who prefers not to say where she served a sentence for knifing another girl, recalls:

'I hated being in prison, cooped up with girls who can be that nasty. I got bullied, then I got into trouble for fighting and there were officers who were mean to me, and rude. I had this cosy picture of my Mum welcoming me home and helping me keep straight, even though she told me when I was sent down she didn't want to know any more. And of course my dream was all wrong: Mum still didn't want to know so I came out to nothing and nobody and suddenly I really wanted to be back inside, I wanted someone to care where I was, to tell me what to do. I felt shit-scared at getting on a train by myself and trying to find my way to the hostel where I had a place.'

Preparing for release

Juveniles

The Youth Justice Board requires that the time a juvenile on a Detention and Training Order (DTO) spends in prison should be coordinated with the subsequent part of their sentence, which is served in the community. A juvenile's Youth Offending Team (YOT) should provide a caseworker whose job it is to visit them inside and help them to consider how they will live their life outside in a way that will prevent them from reoffending. The caseworker should also organise an educational placement or a job for the juvenile to go to on release. At the discretion of the prison governor, a juvenile may be taken, on licence, for job interviews, work placements and college appointments during their time inside. Accommodation must be in place for a juvenile on their release – which can be delayed if it is not. At best children on DTOs feel they have been helped by their caseworkers, and this is particularly true if they receive frequent visits – for example the Hammersmith and Fulham YOT, one of the original pilots, makes two visits a week to each of its YOs.

Tom, 17, who was about to be released from Huntercombe when we met, after a sentence of two years for robbery, felt this way:

'Last time I was inside at a secure unit, I came out and although I had to do a couple of hours a day at a special education unit, most of the time I was hanging out. I got tempted back into crime and as I offended while I was still on licence in the community I was given a long sentence. But here I've done courses with computers and on the internet and my caseworker was really good in getting that sorted so I can do my GNVQ when I'm out. My plan is to do an advanced GNVQ after that. I went for an interview for the college place on resettlement leave with my caseworker. She's been great right through my sentence: when I've asked for something she's really put effort into trying to do it for me. I know she'll be there to support me when I get out. And if anything is going to keep me straight it's that.'

But there are also prisoners who feel their caseworkers have not really been interested, or that they have been, in the words of one, 'just another number on their books, not a person they know'. Dave Seed, in charge of juveniles at Styal, expressed the fairly commonly held view that even with the YOTs up and running, back-up for juveniles is still extremely variable: 'My experience has been that caseworkers are so stretched they can't get to all the sentence planning meetings they should, let alone be as available as the girls need.'

Older young offenders

Whatever the shortcomings of the way in which YOTs work, it is generally agreed that the youth justice reforms have provided a reasonable level of care and support for juveniles. The same cannot be said for 18–21 year olds. There is no statutorily required provision for them, and although prisons are certainly supposed to have a throughcare strategy for older YOs which includes psychological as well as practical preparation for release, whether they do so will depend on the priority given to it by governors and staff, and on the available resources. Richard Garside at Nacro confirms:

> 'One of the biggest problems with current provision for young adults is the lack of preparation for release and inadequate support when they are out. What they get is very haphazard and it is perfectly possible one of this very vulnerable group could find themselves on the pavement with no home or work or education to go to and little idea how to help themselves.'

Some prisons like Moorland and Lancaster Farms do have staff whose job it is to try to find accommodation for young people coming up for release. Likewise some young offender institutions (YOIs) have careers guidance officers working inside, or they may be brought in, but by no means all institutions do this. A problem often voiced is that, since the restructuring of YOIs with the separate juvenile estate, staff who were once available to all YOs must now devote their time to making sure the mandatory hours out of cell and in purposeful activity are observed for 15–17 year olds. This often means there are fewer officers available to do anything for the older YOs, from taking them to pre-release courses or activities to having time to discuss domestic and personal matters that are worrying them prior to their release.

To David Thomas, governor at Lancaster Farms, it is all very unsatisfactory:

> 'These young people inhabit the twilight zone. Many of them are immature, frightened and have no idea how to sort themselves out if there isn't an officer to turn to, yet unless someone chooses to help them they are on their own. And it was not unusual before the YOTs to find probation officers with perhaps 80 in their caseload so presumably they were not going to have much time for sorting out the practical needs of a young person.'

The government has talked of the need for older YOs to receive support similar to that for juveniles, and recently proposed a 'custody plus' sentence for the older age-group, with a fixed time in prison and a compulsory programme in the community, which would offer them a greater sense of direction than at present.[1]

The importance of providing a support and rehabilitation programme for 18–21 year olds that begins inside and continues in the community is clear when you consider that males in this age-group have the highest level of offending – 20% higher than adults. But one of the problems for prisons in dealing with these older YOs is that many are only in for a short time, which means that even with the best intentions little constructive release work can be done. In 1999, more than a quarter of 18–21 year old males and nearly half of females received sentences of three months or less. One governor observed: 'I have some of these kids in just long enough to get their teeth fixed.' Yet even very short sentences often result in loss of accommodation, employment and possibly family ties.

At Moorland, where they have only older YOs and no juveniles, governor Barry McCourt, who replaced David Waplington, brought in Mary Gregory in 2000 to set up a throughcare initiative, Releasing Potential, over three years. This is a wide-ranging plan which incorporates risk-reduction courses, careers guidance and training, skills to equip offenders for employment and a Welfare to Work programme. Sorting out domestic affairs and working with the young people to find accommodation and work placements after release are priorities. Gregory described her plans to me soon after she had arrived:

> 'One of the problems with resettlement in many prisons is that it is

something begun a few weeks before release, but that is very unsatisfactory. You need a strategy to be begun on day one of the sentence so that there is time to sort out difficulties. We realised immediately that we had to concentrate on housing. We have begun to forge links with the communities in the areas where prisoners will be discharged, and the interesting thing is how many companies it turns out are keen to work with ex-offenders. For example Humbercare in Hull have European money for the resettlement of offenders. Doncaster Council are providing a housing worker for us which is a huge help and they deal one-to-one with the young offenders on housing applications right at the beginning of their sentences.

'We are looking at prisoners' timetables and trying to make sure the employment they have in prison is in line with what they want to do outside or what is available. For instance we know in Hull there is a need for skills from catering to fork-lift truck driving, so we might suggest youngsters do an NVQ in one of those. But I also see my job as about influencing hearts and minds. We have to get people outside to take an interest in these young people and see the potential in them because the way they are treated outside has a great deal to do with whether they reoffend.'

At Lancaster Farms, where they take juveniles and the older YOs, David Thomas also believes that resettlement must be part of the general sentence plan. For instance, this might mean trying to retain housing for a young person throughout their sentence, and there is a housing officer who looks into accommodation for this group on release. It might mean getting in touch with the probation officer and discussing family concerns. Personal officers are supposed to be available if a prisoner wants to talk through anxieties about release.

Thomas has focused on basic skills and educational achievement, which he believes will be most useful to YOs when they decide they want to quit crime, as the majority do by the age of 30. However, a recent report by the Howard League criticised the Farms, and other juvenile estate prisons, for putting too much emphasis on formal classroom teaching, rather than on practical, workshop-based activities, providing skills that can be used to earn a living on release. Training, education or work places should be found for young people while they are in custody, so they can see where their efforts are leading, the report argued. And more work should be done to equip them with 'life skills', such as coping on a tight budget, accessing benefits, and basic cooking.[2]

Certainly it is the view of different campaigning organisations that resettlement initiatives for older YOs are unsatisfactory because they depend so much on individual governors, and if a governor who does prioritise this work leaves, the resettlement initiative too often closes down. So these young adults cannot rely on any real preparation for their transition to life outside. As Tim Bateman at Nacro points out, worst practice is an absence of any provision, not bad provision: 'So many units are over capacity so the staff have to direct their energy towards containment rather than considering what happens outside. We are seeing too many youngsters going out pitifully unprepared for trying to lead a law-abiding life outside.'

In 2000 the government's spending review included a £30 million investment by the Prison Service in programmes designed to get more prisoners into accommodation and jobs, so it will be interesting to see if this money will be used to do more for the young adults. The contrast between the efforts made to enable Robbie to emerge from Huntercombe feeling good about himself, and the lack of interest experienced by Peter at Portland when he was there, illustrates as well as anything how important it is that a YOI should have a throughcare programme that works for the inmates.

Robbie tells how at Huntercombe throughcare is seen to start at the beginning of a sentence, with induction, where they look at how time inside will lead to greater possibilities outside. He was given the opportunity, from his first week, to use computers, gain certificates and produce practical work in the form of the prison magazine. 'It meant I had skills, experience and a portfolio when I left', he explained, sitting in the gleaming new shopping precinct in the town where he now lives, sipping hot chocolate and describing his plans to set up his own business. Listening to him you cannot but be struck by the 'can do' confidence he exudes.

When Peter left Portland after an 18-month sentence there was no concern with how he would cope once out. He says:

'The attitude was get your head down and get on with your sentence, that's all we're interested in. So there was no question of turning to any of the officers for help or advice on how you might prepare for life afterwards. Nobody to help us think about the kind of work we might get, what was on offer at colleges. They did give me a Welfare to Work pack but I couldn't make that out, reading's not really my thing. The day I was released I just walked out into nothing which was scary underneath. But on top I was angrier than when I went in because of having to put up with so much humiliation and being pushed about by the screws. It wasn't a very good frame of mind to get myself sorted out.'

Agencies in prison

Across the country, voluntary agencies go into YOIs to help prepare young people for release. Some offer help with finding homes, others work on maintaining family relationships, and there are agencies giving work training and help with employment. The Prison Service is now attempting to 'map' the many small agencies working with YOs to find out what they do and how effective they appear to be.

Nacro runs a small project for under-18 year olds at Portland, looking at their needs after release. It works with the YOTs, trying to help with accommodation and employment if necessary, and may also accompany prisoners home if this support is needed.

One of the larger agencies is the Foundation Training Company, which now operates in four YOIs, offering work skills and help with employment. The charity Outside Chance works with them. Ian Ross, its director, describes his approach when he goes into Feltham shortly before inmates are due for release:

> 'I say it's a bullshit-free course and the common denominator is that you are all here. You've broken into a car, stolen from a house, dealt drugs … whatever. You've done your job of work and you weren't good at it. And what you're up against is that you've had mouth swabs for saliva, you've been finger-printed and you're easy to trace, so your career chances as a criminal are less good than they were. I tell them Outside Chance will do everything it can to help them if they want to go straight and get work, but if they aren't making a genuine commitment to change their offending behaviour we're not interested. Then we look at helping them develop work skills, particularly things like IT which are marketable outside.'

Throughout the past decade the Prince's Trust, working in partnership with social services, the Probation Service, the police, the Prison Service and now the YOTs, has run a young offender self-development course, both inside and outside prison, which focuses on education and training and also on the personal skills that will help YOs overcome the 'multiple blocks' they face in finding employment. The 12-week programme was piloted in 1997 at Hollesley Bay YOI, and by 2001, according to project director Mike Ainsworth, none of the 30 who had taken part in the pilot had been re-convicted, even though not all had got work. The programme is now run in various YOIs. The project works with YOs inside prison for up to eight weeks and they complete the course after release into the community. Interestingly, the Prince's Trust has found that 98% of those referred by prison officers do not reoffend – in other words, when young prisoners feel officers have their best interests at heart it can have a significant impact on their behaviour. With juveniles, 70% of those referred to the Trust by YOTs apparently do not reoffend.

Youth at Risk runs a Coaching for Release course in YOIs, which was piloted at Moorland. It is particularly concerned with tackling the disaffection and alienation of young offenders and getting them to face up to the consequences of their offending, for themselves and their family, the victims and the community. It helps them to develop a sense of responsibility for what they do and to see how they can break the patterns of behaviour that have led them to crime. Youth at Risk works with prisoners in the last two years of their sentence and also holds a series of five-day workshops for prison officers, offenders and volunteers together. There is follow-on support of weekly sessions for a year after release and at the end of the training each young person is allocated a 'committed partner' from the project's volunteers.

The YMCA pioneered its work with YOs under its Partnerships in Prison initiative at Lancaster Farms in 1994, and the programme has since been extended to eight YOIs. It is described as a throughcare programme that is complementary to whatever the prison is doing. The YMCA is concerned with personal development and this is a key ingredient, but also provides basic skills and vocational training. Part of the pre-release work is helping the young people to understand how to search for jobs and how to approach employers, and the YMCA tries to assist in this and to provide accommodation after release. It also encourages prisoners, when they leave, to visit their training centres and other agencies offering support.

On release

The moment of release may have been longed for but many prisoners spoke of how scary it is to find yourself free. In the words of one 17 year old girl: 'You have your life stretching ahead and all the decisions up to you and I just wanted someone to take care of me and tell me what to do at that moment.'

Some prisoners are met by family or friends and taken home, but for those who have nobody it can be very bleak. Even juveniles on DTOs are not met as a matter of course although a YOT worker might decide, in a particular case, to go to the prison. But all under-18s must see their supervising caseworker within a day of release, and after that according to their licence. Older YOs with a sentence of less than four years are assigned a probation officer for three months after they leave prison, or until their 22nd birthday if this is sooner. After sentences of more than four years they are put on parole, which involves longer contact with the Probation Service.

The first thing all over-16 year olds need to do is sign on for benefit, but it takes two weeks for this to be processed, so depending on age YOs are given, on discharge, between £32 and £53 – the equivalent of a week's Income Support or Jobseeker's Allowance. If a prisoner originally came in off the street, or in very worn-out clothing, or if they have lost or gained a lot of weight, they may be given some items of clothing. Those going to a hostel get two towels and young women are given a supply of tampons.

What happens in the first few hours after a young offender is released is crucial, explains Andy Winter, southern coordinator of the YMCA Prisons in Partnership project, who has worked with the YMCA for 20 years and is also a magistrate. The project continues to stay in touch with ex-YOs for as long as they wish:

> 'The first few hours after release are so important, a youngster who feels completely lost and frightened will, quite naturally, gravitate back to friends who he mixed with before. And that may not be the best thing. We aim to help them negotiate the transition from prison to the outside world and one of the things we do which may not sound big but is very significant, is we give them sports bags so they are not having to travel around with a clear plastic sack with all their things inside. When a youngster is released one of our workers accompanies him or her for the first day. Doing that you see how it is for them, feeling so strange, thinking everyone is looking at them, the stress of the first conversations with Mum or another member of the family.'

The possibilities for having a relationship such that an young ex-offender will trust the worker and be motivated to work with them, depend a great deal on the quality of the regime they have experienced and whether they are able to see staff inside as trustworthy, says Larry Wright, manager of the Hammersmith and Fulham YOT. The YOT see their DTO cases twice a week for three months after release, in line with the national standard. But he believes resources are needed to make it possible to see these children as often as they think necessary if they are very needy or vulnerable. Wright, who has conducted his own evaluation of Hammersmith and Fulham's YOT work over a three-month period, has seen reoffending drop by more than 15%. He is now waiting for the results of a national evaluation to see how effective this new way of working with juvenile offenders is.

Agencies

C-Far (the Centre for Adolescent Rehabilitation) runs a post-release scheme which up to now has been able to take only a very limited number of offenders, but which is said by Jo Gordon at the Prison Service to be a model that could usefully be expanded. This is an 11-week residential rehabilitation and resettlement course called Life Change, for YOs from the South-West – many from Portland – who usually attend at the end of their prison sentence. The project was started by Trevor Philpott who, having developed a new approach to training for the Royal Marines which stressed the need for support and encouragement – and for which he won an OBE in 1991 – decided he could apply the same approach to working with persistent YOs. He goes into YOIs and talks about the project – the YOs must volunteer to join it and be motivated enough to give up the time for it after release. The training begins with rigorous outdoor activities designed to encourage 'the lads', as Philpott refers to them, to work together as a team.

This is followed by personal development work, individual counselling, offending behaviour courses, academic education and vocational training. At the end of the course C-Far guarantees the ex-YOs accommodation, an education placement and a mentor for nine months. Although the number of ex-YOs who have been through C-Far since this scheme began in June 2000 is relatively small, they have a lower rate of reoffending than the national average and courses are now oversubscribed.

Peter, a young man whose childhood was a series of family break-downs and attempts to support himself on the street, who has been in and out of prison for property crimes during his teens, went to C-Far from Port-land. He found the course hard because he was accustomed to using anger and antisocial behaviour when things got difficult in life:

> 'I didn't find it easy having to open up and talk about my life and feel-ings and that, and I wasn't sure I wanted to stay. You don't have to, you've finished your sentence, so nobody is going to force you. One evening I got upset about something and got very angry, kicking off all over the place. Then I decided I'd leave so I strode off to the gate but as I was getting there I found myself thinking "Where does it leave me if I go? I'm angry but I can choose not to be angry." That was some-thing we had discussed in one of the groups – so I turned round, went back and apologised to the member of staff I'd had a row with. That was a very valuable lesson for me because I'd never thought about controlling my anger before – there never seemed any point. Once I'd got through that I started a catering course, something I'd always wanted to do, and now I'm working in catering and living in a house C-Far found for me with my partner and baby.'

Outside Chance encourages young people it has worked with in Feltham to visit its office after release. If all they want is a chat, a bit of company and some support, that is on offer. But director Ian Ross sees his mission as helping ex-YOs to get work. He recalls one young man who had done well on the IT course in prison and had good keyboard skills. Soon after he was released he arrived at the office and started looking through job advertise-ments in the newspapers there. He circled one for a keyboard operator:

> 'We suggested he try for an interview, if only for practice. He wrote off after this job and asked me to check the letter. A few days later he returned to the office with a standard letter sent to applicants and he had been longlisted for interview. We knew he had to be helped to feel confident. So I lent him a suit – we keep several in the cupboard given to a local reject shop by companies like Gap. I also had shirts and ties from a local charity shop, but then out of the kitty we bought him a new pair of shoes and socks so that he felt well dressed. I offered to

take him to the interview but he said he could cope. Ten days later he appeared, he was shaking, and he told me he had got the job.'

Clean Break was set up by two women prisoners from Askham Grange in 1979 to offer a free theatre education to women coming out of prison. It is open to all women aged over 16 years, but 50% of those who come to the day centre in London, and often keep attending for months or years, are under 24. Today Clean Break, which works closely with the Probation Service, runs a range of accredited and NVQ courses to do with theatre work, drama and literacy and is keen to get as many women as possible into work. But, explains education director Fay Barratt, as importantly, it provides space where women can be with each other, gain confidence and explore their creativity as a way of 'getting back to life' after prison. Clean Break also puts on touring productions, often with ex-offenders performing.

Accommodation

Barty, 18, had left prison several months before we met. He was living in a flat in North London and was on Jobseeker's Allowance. He said, emphatically, that he did not want to go back into crime, and certainly not to return to prison. He thought he could manage to stay straight '… so long as I have my home. If I lost that, then I might slip …'

Of all the things that play a part in preventing offending or reoffending housing is absolutely central. The Chief Inspector of Prisons' thematic review of YOs found that on reception to prison 'approximately 25% of young prisoners are homeless, or have been in insecure accommodation.[3] Nacro's own 1998 survey of 45 YOs found that 60% had experienced unstable living conditions.[4]

A 1986 Home Office review of research is to date the most definitive report of the link between homelessness and reoffending. One survey it looked at found that of 600 released male prisoners less than a third who had homes to go to were reconvicted over a two-year period, compared with 69% of prisoners with no homes.[5] On the basis of this survey Nacro estimates that a homeless ex-prisoner is twice as likely to reoffend as a housed one. Home Office research in 1999 found that reconviction among those on community sentence was also consistently higher for those with accommodation problems.[6]

Some young prisoners, of course, have family homes to return to but there are a considerable number who are in rented accommodation and with tenancies which may expire during their time inside. The chances of most of them being able to keep paying rent during even a short custodial sentence are small and housing benefit can be paid by the state for only 13 weeks for a sentenced prisoner, so these prisoners are likely to lose the home they had before custody – the place that quite possibly provides them with the one piece of security and stability they have. It is one of the most damaging impacts of a prison sentence, and it seems a particularly high price to pay if the sentence is short and for a relatively minor crime. And while most young people have difficulties finding affordable accommodation in a market that usually has a shortage, or landlords prepared to take an age-group often seen as more trouble than mature adults, it is not difficult to see how much harder it is for ex-offenders to do so. Local authorities have a statutory obligation to meet the housing needs of older ex-YOs only if they can show 'extreme vulnerability'.

YOTs are in a position to help juveniles with their housing costs. Hammersmith and Fulham YOT, for example, managed by Larry Wright, has a housing manager who endeavours to keep rents paid if the sentence is not too long. However, a homeless juvenile is the responsibility of the local authority, although that often means they are put into bed and breakfast accommodation, which can be a very unsatisfactory situation for a young person in need of some care and back-up. Wright's team is looking for funding for extra staff to support those in such accommodation. He is also particularly proud of their work with a social landlord who is building a young persons' eight-bed hostel which will function as a halfway house. These are good models of practice that other YOTs could follow.

There are additional problems for ex-YOs aged between 18 and 24 because they receive £11 a week less Income Support than those who are 25 and over, even though their living costs are likely to be the same. And housing benefit for under-25s is restricted to the rent of a single room.[7] The assumption here is that under-25s can rely on their parents, but in fact many cannot. The young man whose mother died when he was in his early teens and who put himself into care because he could not get on with his stepmother is one. In an adult prison where he was one of very few YOs he brooded about how he would cope when released: 'I studied hard in prison so I knew I could get to college, but I had no idea how I would find a place to live. I've friends who went to hostels and bed and breakfast because there wasn't anything else, but they were grim and chaotic. There's no way I'd be able to study in a place like that.'

A particularly inhumane situation exists for women whose children have been taken into care or who are looked after by relatives: they are judged childless by housing authorities and so do not have priority for housing. Without a home they may not be able to regain custody of their child. Again, given the short sentences most women receive for their mainly non-violent offences, this loss is often far harsher than the term of punishment they serve to pay for their offence.

A number of voluntary organisations offer ex-offenders hostel places. The YMCA is the largest provider of housing for young people with more than 6,000 bed spaces around the country and it claims it will not turn an ex-YO away. Other organisations and the Probation Service also run hostels and ex-YOs can apply for housing association homes. Some hostels are clearly good with efficient and supportive carers on site, but others, like the one Liz went to, after Holloway and Bulwood Hall, are not: 'I was put in a place where I didn't trust anyone. Half of them was ex-offenders like me. For days I just kept the door closed and blocked it. In a way it was like being back in my cell, but lonelier and I got very depressed.'

Robbie, who had been detoxed at Huntercombe, knew he had to get out of the hostel where he had been placed by the prison:

'I'd spent a lot of my young life in prison and for the first time, partly because I had a long sentence, I'd got clean and had a chance to think about my life. At Huntercombe I got skills and I came out believing I could go straight. But then I arrived at my hostel and found it was full of people like me who had lived by crime and a lot were straight back on drugs once they got through the prison gates. There were dealers coming in all the time. I knew I had to get out if I didn't want to get sucked back in. I was lucky I got a job in a bar and earned enough to rent myself a place in the town and that's been great.'

Robbie's story illustrates well the potential problems of putting vulnerable young people into accommodation without being sure it is supportive of their needs. The inspirational Foyer movement was set up in recognition of the problems faced by many young people, including ex-YOs. The Foyer Federation brings together under one umbrella, though not necessarily in one place, affordable accommodation, guidance and support and help in accessing education, training and employment.

Young Builders Trust (YBT) initiatives offer ex-YOs, and other young people in difficult circumstances, not only housing but employment, marketable skills and often a level of self-esteem they have never experienced. The Trust works with local authorities and housing associations to buy up derelict houses or pieces of land for development and to raise funds for materials to renovate old houses or to build new ones. Ex-YOs, often referred through the Probation Service or by youth justice workers, join a team of around six others to build or renovate houses which they can then rent, with their housing benefit if they do not immediately find work. (They are eligible to claim benefit during the building work.) Most have no building skills when they begin, but there is a training manager on site, and they also attend college where they work towards formal building qualifications. The idea is that these young people will become well equipped to earn a living in building or some allied trade at a time when the construction industry needs to recruit more than double the number of trainees it currently has. In the scheme, groups of young people tend to work on several homes at once, often in the same area, so they may form a community who already know each other when they come to rent the houses. The YBT has applied to run a pilot Youthbuild scheme for prisoners in Feltham. It will have four stages: recruitment, pre-vocational training in prison, then experience under licensed release to the potential employer followed by formal employment with the contractor on release.

The difference such imaginative schemes can make to a YO's life is heard in the tale of an ex-YO who was winner of the National Youthbuild Awards in 2000: 'My mother threw me out of home because I could not get on with my stepfather. I was unemployed so I had no money to rent a place. I slept for several nights on a train station then got a bed at a night shelter, but I didn't feel very safe and I was very depressed.' He was put in touch with the YBT and they offered him the chance to work with them:

> 'I'd only ever done portering work so I didn't have a clue about carpentry and joinery, but the training manager and support worker really built my confidence and wouldn't let me give up. I was anxious about doing the theory because I got bullied at school and hated it, so I was very scared I would fail. But I enjoyed it and it was the first time I felt good about anything I did. At college I learnt to use a computer, finished my NVQ1 after a month and received an NVQ2 in carpentry and joinery and level one in word processing. It's changed my life completely. I now have a full-time job, a tenancy and a home where I feel safe. I find it easier to get on with my family and I'm engaged to marry.'

Even when young prisoners do have family homes these may not be the best places for them to return to. Prison staff know well how chaotic, abusive and dangerous have been the environments many of their charges come from. Or these homes may be in areas where the prisoner's peers are criminalised or drug users, and it will be all too easy for the young person to slip back into their company. One prison officer at Moorland said despairingly:

> 'I've got close to some of our lads and felt really optimistic about their chances, but then we're told they've got a home to go to and off they are sent to a place where there's an alcoholic parent, or one I can think of where the lad was sodomised throughout his childhood. Or there's complete neglect which means the kid has no boundaries and no respect for anyone – often what got him into trouble in the first place. So off he's sent and guess what, we get him back within a very short time. I find myself thinking, "put that kid in a different environment with people to keep an eye on him and he'll have a chance".'

Isn't it ridiculous, demands John Harding, former director of the Inner

London Probation Service, that 'huge amounts of money are spent on secure places for children and young people, but that money does not follow them outside?' He reflects:

> 'Some of the best places, where they do high-intensity work with the young people or really try to care for them, are expensive to run but they can do some positive and hopeful work with their inmates. But that money is thrown away because so many are discharged without a good enough accommodation plan and if that is not sorted out then how can you can make progress? It may seem reasonable to ask these young people to get things straight for themselves but we need to stop and consider what incredible stamina, commitment and discipline that takes. All of which we might expect of a child who has been raised by loving disciplined parents although even they can foul up, but the risk with these vulnerable youngsters is obviously much greater.'

Work

In the YOIs I visited, plenty of inmates had a done a sentence or more before the one they were currently serving. And repeatedly I heard that they reoffended after losing a job or when a short-term contract had ended, putting paid to the dreams they share with so many of us of buying a house, marrying, having children and even, as one young man put it, 'being able to dress like a toff and have a really flash holiday'. George, 17, completing a second sentence for robbery, had had a job plastering for three months after his first spell in prison, but that had ended and he found it impossible to get another job, not least because when employers heard about his record they 'never rang back'. He was broke and bored, and very quickly looked up the friends he had avoided mixing with when he left prison and was employed.

The link between unemployment and offending is also well established. Research in this country and in the US shows that ex-offenders are less likely to be reconvicted if they are employed,[8] and of course many young people inevitably lose their jobs when they are sent down. The Prison Service is a partner in the government's Welfare to Work initiative, which is designed to get young people off benefit and into work. This ties in with the New Deal, set up to help 18–24 year olds, and run by the DfES, which coordinates companies, training providers such as colleges, training and enterprise councils, local authorities, job centres, and voluntary groups. Unemployed young people are appointed a local New Deal personal adviser to help them work out what they want to do, and to put them in touch with other agencies. Some YOIs bring in New Deal advisers to work with YOs before release, but this is at the discretion of the governor. YOT teams also work with the advisers.

After education, which breaks through the illiteracy and innumeracy barrier and which ideally engages the interest and enthusiasm of young prisoners, giving training that will provide them with a marketable skill is one of the most valuable things prison can do. But the training offered in YOIs varies hugely. For example, industrial cleaning, low-grade manufacturing and hairdressing are easy for prisons to provide, but are considered by such critics as Chris Tchaikovsky, director of Women in Prison, to be 'very basic stuff with low expectations of what these prisoners can do'. Practical and popular courses are car maintenance, music technology, printing, high-standard painting and decorating classes, horticulture and catering. Health, hygiene and safety are frequently part of training. At Holloway, gardening is one of the most imaginative of pre-release work opportunities, providing unusual skills and winning an award for the inmates. Most YOIs now offer IT training and this is one area which can put YOs who have a flair for it on an equal footing with other job applicants, even though they may lack other academic qualifications.

Nacro and the Apex Trust are two organisations which understand how doubly disadvantaged young ex-offenders are if they emerge from time inside with no marketable skills and no idea what they could learn to do. Both concentrate on helping people with criminal records to gain skills and find work. Another such organisation is the Prince's Trust, which through its Acorn project helps ex-YOs start their own businesses – liaising with the Probation Service to assess who might be eligible for a start-up loan. Bruce, 21, trained in prison to do window cleaning and worked with another ex-offender when he came out. They began to get business and were given a loan to buy equipment. They now own their own company, employ two other people and have as much work as they can manage. The pleasing irony of what this means is not lost on Bruce, who was inside for taking and driving away cars and has now been able to buy himself a BMW.

But however well ex-prisoners may have done in developing marketable skills they still have to overcome the prejudice of employers who will not take on someone with a criminal record – equal opportunities policies that acknowledge the rights of ex-offenders are rare. Suzanna watched her son James apply for IT jobs, for which he was well qualified, and advised him to be honest about his criminal record – six months in a YOI for possessing and selling cannabis. James's experience was typical: 'He just never heard back. Employers would see him for an interview and he'd tell them what he'd been doing immediately before and they would say they'd be in touch. But they never got back to James.'

A number of projects have attempted to beat such prejudice. South Glamorgan Probation Service, together with the careers service, ran a positive initiative to raise awareness among employers of the issues around the training and employment of ex-offenders and to help employers see how they could use ex-YOs. Another initiative was launched in 1999 by Nacro: Going Straight to Work brought together a group of leading employers, including Tesco, the CBI, and the TUC, to spearhead a drive to overcome discrimination against ex-offenders and to help employers realistically assess the risks in employing them. The project is still running and Nacro plans to publish a guide with recruitment advice for employers.

I heard of two encouraging proactive initiatives by staff in YOIs that could well be replicated by others. At Deerbolt YOI, two prison officers started a small-business course with funding from local firms. The firms sent staff into the prison to discuss the course with the YOs and subsequently employed two of them after they had left prison – they later went on to start businesses of their own. And at Thorn Cross YOI the catering instructor spotted that there were a lot of jobs in catering available around the country, many also providing accommodation, and encouraged the young inmates to apply. He accompanied YOs to interviews and made sure their training matched the job requirements.

Family

Jacob, 20, became distanced from his parents as his drug addiction took him over and his need for money to feed his habit drove him to steal. Eventually he took his father's credit card and drew out several thousand pounds. When his father realised what had happened he went to the police and Jacob was arrested:

> 'My parents and I had been getting on badly because with the drugs I became more and more distant and impossible and I'd moved out of home. It was terrible for them seeing me sent to prison because they had gone ahead with charges and I couldn't believe it. But all through my prison sentence they wrote and visited me and explained that they knew they had to do something to stop me. As I detoxed inside I began to feel such pain at what I had done to them and so grateful that they hadn't given up on me. When I was leaving I knew I had a home to go to, and the irony is that we're closer now than before and I feel I could tell them if I got into difficulties next time.'

The importance of a strong and supportive family in helping YOs stay away from crime was stressed by just about everyone I spoke to who works with them. There was general agreement on what needs doing. Ideally parents should be involved as much as possible in working for and with their children in sentence planning. The view was often expressed that parenting courses could help families support their children when they get into trouble. Prisons and YOTs need to do all they can to maintain or rebuild family links, and given how difficult and delicate prison visits can be, should ensure that visiting facilities are appealing, that prisoners are given all possible privacy, and that visiting times are as flexible as possible. But as important as any of these is that the courts avoid putting so many young people into YOIs when the nearest available places may be far from where they live – this happens a great deal and many parents cannot afford the time off work, childcare cover or fares to visit their children.

Parents who do visit regularly and are consistent in keeping commitments to their young are certainly helpful in rehabilitating them, but often it is not like this, as David Thomas explains:

> 'The thing I am disappointed in is family links. I have worked at them because they have a real effect on delinquency even when they are the most difficult families. We would like to be able to do far more in the way of whole-family education because families that don't understand the damaging things that may be going on between them or what their child's problem is, may not be able to offer the support needed when the young offender goes home. But without extra resources it's not possible for us to do that.'

At Hammersmith and Fulham Larry Wright heads a YOT where family relationships are a priority. He says:

> 'The madness of a custodial sentence for kids, unless really essential, is that it can break family relationships which cannot always be rebuilt, but we do work with families to try to repair difficult situations and the importance of parents coming to planning meetings is that the child sees they care enough, which has a lot of symbolic meaning particularly if things have been difficult between them. My staff will bring parents to meetings and travel back with them, because that is a time to look at what has happened in the meeting. Of course some parents are far from ideal although it is not always their fault that life may be very difficult and stressful. But children often want, against huge odds, to have a relationship with their parent or parents so we work with the reality of that, helping the child understand what goes on. We don't pretend the home situation is better than it is.'

Listening to young people describing the pain and confusion of family life and relations with parents, it is clear that prison may sometimes provide a respite and an opportunity for rebuilding.

Suzanna described how her son James went downhill after the death of his adored stepfather. Absorbed in her own grief and caring for her son by her dead husband, she became increasingly estranged from James. He in turn became withdrawn and defiant, and as he reached his teens he dropped out of school and spent more and more time on the street:

'I thought he was depressed and tried to get help, but there wasn't any and I couldn't afford to pay privately ... By the time he was sent to prison he had been in trouble with the law several times, but that was bad – very bad. He was very frightened and he made it clear he did not think I cared about him. It took that to make me realise how badly I had let him down and how much he needed me as a mother. I wrote to him just about every day and I visited every possible time and we began to talk about what had happened, what he had been going through. By the time James came out we were very close, he knew I loved him, and that he had a home to come to. I think for both of us prison provided a space in which we could begin anew and James has been studying and working since he came home.'

Sometimes seeing their children in prison is the catalyst to parents recognising where *they* have gone wrong. When Sam was given life for murdering his mother and sent to Moorland, his father Ronald was very clear that he would try to be as supportive of his son as he could: 'I wanted to be the parent I should have been when he was outside. I let Sam down badly by breaking up the family and not seeing how he was feeling. Instead I ruled him with fear and shut myself away from knowing what he needed as a child.' He reflects on his disciplinarian views that went as far as taking Sam to police cells as a child, to show him 'where he would end up' if he got into trouble. He preached honesty and decency but, when Sam was 13, he left his wife for another woman, not seeing how devastated Sam was or how much responsibility he took on, living alone with his very depressed mother:

'I can't undo that but I can show Sam I have changed and that above all I want to be a loving father who he can turn to when he needs to. We don't do a great deal of deep talking, it's more a case of my visiting him very regularly, picking up on problems, letting him know I am there and he is absolutely the most important thing in my life.

'I have learnt that he likes to hear about what I have been doing, what has been happening, then he tells me about his education – he's very keen on computers and he is doing Shakespeare now – and what he wants to do in the future. But one of the best things is that I have been allowed to attend what is called his 'lifer assessment' session – he's on a lifer course doing anger management, self-awareness and such things – where he discusses what happened and it can be a struggle, painful for him, but I am grateful to be brought in on this. It's part of a lifer day.'

And Sam, sitting with me in a room on the enhanced wing, where he has earned a place through good behaviour, says:

'At first when I got arrested I didn't want to see my Dad. I was too scared to confront him and getting close is still difficult on visits. He comes once a fortnight and writes letters occasionally. We talk but there are a lot of things I feel I can't say to him and I don't want to upset him. He finds it hard to express himself and sometimes I feel I don't know him at all. But I'm glad he's there for me because I do love him.'

Prison may be a time when young people recognise how their crime has damaged their family life. Loocie, 17, found herself considering this at Holloway:

'I found myself thinking about things that had never crossed my mind before because I did everything on autopilot. Things like my attitudes and how I behaved when I was on heroin. I was shooting up every day and committing crime – a lot of shoplifting – to get the money. My being an addict split my Mum and stepdad up. Now I know I just want to get out and keep out of trouble.'

For children like Loocie learning to cope without family can be hard, as Lorraine Holt, senior officer at Styal when I visited, saw repeatedly. She referred to a recent case:

'A girl left yesterday with no family, just going to a hostel. She's been on drugs and I imagine she'll go back to them because there's nobody to help her, to make her feel she matters. It breaks my heart when they start telling me before they go that they don't want to leave, they ask if they can phone me and of course I say yes. But I feel desperate for them – I think of my kids and how it is family life that holds them safe.'

For many parents of children and young people in prison, the feelings of shame and isolation can make it still harder for them to parent well. Suzanna realised she was not alone in her suffering when she began to talk with other mothers of YOs. It was this that inspired her to set up a support group for mothers of children in trouble with the law and in prison. She says:

'People feel quite desperate when these things are happening, they can be angry, they can turn against their child, they may wonder how they can ever face the neighbours when their child comes home. But when we meet and talk and understand we are all in it together, things seem easier. We share information, help each other cope and know what to do if something bad happens to one of our children inside. We take care of anyone who is very upset, and we have a helpline so that people can ring at any time if they feel desperate. As I know, being a good parent to a child in prison can be the thing that saves them, but we parents need help too.'

They do not want to return

Repeatedly in conversation young people voiced their determination not to get into trouble again and return to prison, not always because they saw the folly of their ways but because they did not want to lose their freedom again. In the words of Jake, 18, at Lancaster Farms: 'I know I've got to stop because I've seen where my path leads. There are these guys who have been in and out of prison all their lives, they lose their homes, their wives, their kids. They grow old in prison – it's not for me.'

Yet overwhelmingly they do reoffend – close to 90% of the juveniles – and many return to prison. The reasons have been documented here – not having a proper home, inability to get work, loneliness and falling back into a peer group who are sometimes the only people they see as friends. But one of the reasons they may return, which makes Steive Butler at Huntercombe particularly angry, is when they are charged with crimes committed before the sentence just served. She explains:

'We work to rehabilitate them here, get them sorted so they just may be able to manage not to slip back into crime when they are released. And what happens? They get picked up by the police and taken back to court for an offence, and often a very small one, which happened before they got arrested and sent here. So back they come and our job is that much harder the next time. It makes no sense at all and it certainly doesn't benefit the public.'

Of all that is wrong with the prison experience for YOs, it is clear that it is absence of support after release, especially for older YOs, that makes it so difficult for them to go on to lead constructive lives. And if they have lost their homes, cannot find work because of their prison record, and family relationships have broken down, it is as though, having got through their official punishment, they are punished all over again.

NOTES

1. *Criminal Justice: The way ahead*. London, Home Office, 2001.
2. *Children in Prison: Provision and practice at Lancaster Farms*. London, Howard League for Penal Reform, 2001.
3. *Young Prisoners: A thematic review by HM Chief Inspector of Prisons for England and Wales*. London, Home Office, 1997.
4. *Wasted Lives: Counting the cost of juvenile offending*. London, Nacro, 1998.
5. Malcolm Ramsay, *Housing for the Homeless Ex-offender: Key findings from a literature review*, Home Office Research Bulletin 20. London, Home Office, 1986.

6. C. May, *Explaining Reconviction Following a Community Sentence: The role of social factors,* Home Office Research Study 192. London, Home Office, 1999.
7. *Young Adult Offenders: A period of transition.* London, Nacro, 2001.
8. Penny Robson, Home Office Chief Education Officer, speaking in 2000 at the conference 'A Second Chance: The employment and training of children with criminal records', hosted by the Michael Sieff Foundation.

Final thoughts

Visiting prisons, talking with young inmates, I was repeatedly struck by the poignant truth of child therapist Bruno Bettelheim's observation that 'if children are reared so that life is meaningful to them, they will not need special help'. Meaning is conspicuously lacking in the lives of most of the young we lock away. With few exceptions, the stories I heard of young offenders' lives before they became delinquent and turned to crime were of chaos, distress, neglect and often severe disadvantage. They did indeed feel a sense of futility and meaninglessness, and had frequently turned to drugs or alcohol as a way of blotting out these bad feelings. Crime, particularly when it was committed with a close-knit peer group, gave life a spurious kind of meaning, a 'buzz', as they described it.

Yet so many of the young people I met had a lot of potential: sharp wits, inspiration, creativity, humour, a formidable survival instinct, an understanding of human psychology. I found myself thinking how much society would have benefited – indeed still could benefit – if those qualities had been channelled into constructive use rather than into committing crimes. Not that committing crimes made those I spoke to particularly happy. On the whole, they would rather not be criminals, though for some it was a source of kudos, and most did not want to spend their lives in and out of prison. The trouble was that they had few ideas of how they could make a go of a more conventional, conformist life, and were often ill-equipped to do so.

Most young offenders come from the bottom of the social scale, and are likely to have grown up with crushing deprivation and all the social and educational problems it brings. That is not to say that kids who go wrong do so because of their social status – this is not original sin with a class bias – but society should recognise these predisposers to crime and become concerned about trying to provide better support services for children and families at risk. Jack Straw, when Home Secretary, made much of his intention to be tough on the causes of crime, and addressing these with greatly increased commitment and resources must surely be a more humane and effective way of preventing crime than by locking up ever more young offenders. Prison is an expensive way of failing to get the results we want. Currently, over 75% of young ex-offenders are reconvicted, usually within a short time of leaving prison, and if you include those who do not get caught the figure for reoffending is almost certainly nearer 90%. So imprisoning young criminals is not an efficient way to rehabilitate them or to protect the public.

Yet, ironically, the best prison regimes are able to discover and develop some of the potential of young inmates in a way that has generally not happened before in their lives and may actually enable them to find meaning, choose to learn skills that give them a choice about whether to return to crime or not and, as important as anything, to learn that adults may be with them rather than against them. It is grimly ironic, too, how many of the young I spoke with said that they were glad to have come to prison because they could not have got themselves out of the spiral of chaos and crime they were in without being physically removed from it, in many cases detoxed, and being obliged to live in a different way. Others simply found prison life easier to cope with than life outside.

This should not be read as an advertisement for prison. Even the best of regimes do not alter the fact that prison by its very nature is in many ways destructive and negative. There are undoubtedly young people who need to be removed from their communities and to live an entirely different life for long enough to break their pattern of crime. But we should question whether it is necessary for so many non-violent young offenders to be locked up in order to receive this sort of help and rehabilitation. Imagine if the money spent on incarcerating such young people was used instead to create rehabilitation centres in the community which young offenders had to attend all day, with a high staff-to-pupil ratio, providing education, skills training, offending behaviour courses, as well as arts, sports training, and accommodation if necessary. Such places would not carry the stigma of prison, nor result in a prison record, but could offer the best rehabilitative aspects of a good prison regime.

Restorative justice, restoring the balance disturbed by crime, is an approach that is being seen as having much to offer in the rehabilitation process. This may involve mediation between the victim and offender, either indirectly, or directly in a structured meeting, or in group conferences also involving family, community members and relevant professionals. The aim is that the offender should own responsibility for their crime, be made aware of the effect it has had on the victim and as a result reassess their future behaviour. Although often seen as a soft option for offenders, this process can in fact be difficult for them and has the potential to be more satisfactory for victims, in terms of offering them an explanation, an apology and some form of reparation.[1]

Community work also offers a useful alternative to prison, whether in this country or abroad with, for example, development aid postings. One young man I met who had previously just embarked on criminal activity of a non-violent kind was helped to raise the money to go to work in a hospital in Bangladesh where for the first time he felt valued. He returned to the UK and trained to be a nursery worker. Another young person I spoke to, who had narrowly escaped prison, instead spent six months care-taking special needs teenagers in a hostel. After working with people more needy than himself he too emerged with a sense of his own worth. There are of course many such good community schemes already in place region-ally and the number of these should be increased.

Government should also spend money on offering young people leaving prison the support and help they require to find a home, and an education place or a job. Mentors are much talked about at present and certainly for these youngsters who so often have nobody to turn to and rely on the odd phone call to their prison officer, they seem a very good idea. The cost of employing people of the right calibre and commitment to do this work would surely be cheaper than sending reoffenders back to prison.

For such community sentences and projects to be successful in rehabilitating young people who offend, society needs to understand the backgrounds they come from and see the value of taxes being spent this way. If we stop to consider the kind of circumstances we want our children to grow up in, the opportunities we feel will help them to function well, the kindness and caring we know to be essential to their psychological well-being, and then consider how absent these things are in the lives of those who go on to offend against us, it is easier to understand why humanity demands that we try to offer them something more nurturing. In this context the words of the eminent psychiatrist Anthony Storr have real resonance: 'The child who has never felt cared for, will care for nobody.' If we can help these young people to feel cared for and thus to care, before they harden into criminalised adults, it will be better for all of us.

Many people equate concern for young offenders with lack of concern for victims. I would argue that the two go hand in hand. Concern for victims also means that, as a society, we have to involve ourselves more with the young who offend against them. We have the means, through our voices, our votes, our taxes and our concern, to change the conditions in which those most likely to go on to offend spend their early years. It is time for society to understand that children in general should be the responsibility of all of us and that we must be active in helping them, and their families when necessary, if we are going to lock them up in the name of society when they go wrong.

NOTE
1. Roger Graef, *Why Restorative Justice? Repairing the harm caused by crime*. London, Calouste Gulbenkian Foundation, 2001.

Index